CONGRESS BEHAVING BADLY

CONGRESS BEHAVING BADLY

The Rise of Partisanship and Incivility and the Death of Public Trust

SUNIL AHUJA

Foreword by Former Congressman Tom Sawyer

Westport, Connecticut
London

Library of Congress Cataloging-in-Publication Data

Ahuja, Sunil.
  Congress behaving badly : the rise of partisanship and incivility and the death
  of public trust / Sunil Ahuja ; foreword by Tom Sawyer.
    p. cm.
  Includes bibliographical references and index.
  ISBN 978–0–275–99868–4 (alk. paper)
1. United States. Congress—History—20th century. 2. United States.
Congress—History—21st century. 3. United States—Politics and government—
1945–1989. 4. United States—Politics and government—1989– 5. Etiquette—
United States. 6. Political culture—United States. I. Title.
JK1041.A48 2008
328.73—dc22   2007045054

British Library Cataloguing in Publication Data is available.

Library of Congress Catalog Card Number: 2007045054
ISBN: 978–0–275–99868–4

First published in 2008

Praeger Publishers, 88 Post Road West, Westport, CT 06881
An imprint of Greenwood Publishing Group, Inc.
www.praeger.com

Printed in the United States of America

∞

The paper used in this book complies with the
Permanent Paper Standard issued by the National
Information Standards Organization (Z39.48-1984).

10 9 8 7 6 5 4 3 2 1

The author and publisher gratefully acknowledge the use of excerpts from the
following sources:

Fight Club Politics: How Partisanship is Poisoning the House of Representatives, by
Juliet Eilperin, with the permission of the publisher, Hoover Institution Press.
Copyright 2006 by the Board of Trustees of the Leland Stanford Junior University.

Thomas E. Mann and Norman J. Ornstein, *The Broken Branch: How Congress Is
Failing America and How to Get It Back on Track* (New York: Oxford University
Press, 2006). By permission of Oxford University Press, Inc.

To My Parents
Nand and Sadhana Ahuja

CONTENTS

FOREWORD

In the spring of 1992, a stunned nation watched as massive civil disturbance spread throughout South Central Los Angeles, triggered by a brutal, failed traffic arrest that ignited days of looting, destruction of property, and racial and ethnic conflict that horrified all who saw it. And when it was over, the battered arrest victim, Rodney King, posed his still indelible plea, "Why can't we all just get along?"

It was a poignant and memorable appeal. However, South Central L.A., as the event came to be known, was the product of a far more complex mixture of economic, demographic, and migratory pressures than the question suggests. And understanding it requires more than answering Rodney King's question.

South Central L.A. was full of contradictions, tensions, and competitions of a kind likely to tear any community apart under the right circumstance.

And so when, in the closing pages of *Congress Behaving Badly*, author Sunil Ahuja poses a similar plea (" . . . for members of Congress to get along"), it has a distressingly familiar ring. But like L.A., Congress is far more complex than the King lament suggests. It is a useful question, but it is not sufficient.

Actually on approaching this book with the thought of writing a foreword, I did not much like it. At least not at first. I thought it was superficial. I was wrong.

I have been an elected official for most of the past thirty years, sixteen of them in the U.S. Congress during some of the most turbulent years described in *Congress Behaving Badly*. I have lived this book.

Congress Behaving Badly captures observations of, and about, the contemporary Congress in its multiple facets, by a wide range of commentators including journalists and scholars, as well as a large sampling of elected members of Congress themselves, most of whom I have known well.

They do not paint a pretty picture, and perhaps they should not. But I have grown tired of criticisms aimed at the symptoms of uncivil behavior as detailed in many of the early commentaries included in this book. And the whole catalogue of causes for these conditions sometimes seems altogether too petty to have hamstrung the Constitution's first branch of government.

(I am for my own part always a little irked to observe that journalists invariably report legislative stories in partisan terms. Political reporting typically defines battle lines between sides on legislation, tallying win-loss scores on bills, even identifying legislative members in partisan shorthand—Tom Sawyer, D-Ohio—in ways seldom done with executive office holders. It is less complicated than writing about the nuance of substantive debate, even when it would help to illuminate an issue. As one who has been both the mayor of a midsize American city—Akron, OH—and its member of Congress, I can testify to the difference. It is a pet peeve.)

So I had largely determined with Gary Orren (see chapter 5) not to cast my lot with the "public officials, who themselves ceaselessly demean each other and the very institutions in which they serve," and therefore, not to write this foreword.

As I continued to read, however, what emerged was not a garden variety rant against a Congress whose "highlight reels" are telecast live and hashed over endlessly throughout the 24-hour news cycle. Nevertheless, much of the text is drawn from criticisms of that kind.

However, this book is not merely a lamentation for a devoutly to be wished, but long lost legislative body. Rather, *Congress Behaving Badly* portrays a complex governmental body in an era of transition and turmoil. It is much more than a lamentation.

Congress, in one way or another, has always reflected the good and the bad in our national fabric. The 1950s and 1960s may have been a more "civil" time in Congress as the author suggests. It was a quieter time in America as well. But it was also a time of quiet tolerance of conditions that today we view as intolerable, from McCarthyism to Jim Crow and more.

And the post–World War 1940s, now often forgotten, are characterized by congressional scholar Kathleen Hall Jamieson as the equal to the 1990s in quantifiable measures of member to member incivility in the conduct of congressional business. The numbers of times the chamber had to be gaveled to silence, incidences of members' words being officially stricken from the record, the banishment of members themselves from the floor of the chamber for a time, and other recorded cases of "Congress Behaving Badly" were, in the several congresses following World War II, fully the equal of the current era.

Like now, it was a time of enormous social, demographic, technological, and economic change in America.

Millions of men had come home from war. The Baby Boom exploded. (No prime time TV at first. Couples had to do *something!*) And then there was TV itself. And cars, cars, cars. Economic boom on one hand and nuclear cold war on the other. Congressional majorities and administrations shifted.

And like now, the resulting turmoil played itself out in the body politic, most visibly in Congress where members reacted with a combativeness similar to that of today but without the opportunity to play to gavel-to-gavel coverage on C-SPAN.

The current era is similar in striking ways.

The leadership and majorities in both chambers have shifted several times within recent years, during administrations of presidents of both parties.

It has also been a time of enormous technological change:

- 20 years ago mobile phones, for the few who had them, were carried in briefcases or the center consoles of cars;
- 20 years ago the Internet did not exist for everyday use;
- 20 years ago, for most Americans, the news came at 6:30 PM on three networks.

And in 1986, if an interviewer had asked any candidate for Congress, incumbent or challenger, to discuss the likely global strategic dynamic 20 years hence, the universal answer would have described a continuing nuclear standoff between the Soviet Bloc and the Western Alliance, held in place by the certainty of mutual assured destruction. Anyone who had replied that in five years there would be no Soviet Union would have been deemed unfit to serve. And yet, that is precisely what happened. The Czech playwright, Vaclav Havel, who became his country's president, remarked in an address to a joint session of Congress that change "had come so suddenly, we did not have time even to be astonished."

At the same time, large economic and demographic shifts propelled political and social changes of tectonic magnitude across a complex nation. Those changes and the resulting tensions are inevitably reflected in the conduct and culture of the body elected to represent that complex and shifting society.

When we look at the nation through the prism of the Congress we have elected, we have much to learn from *Congress Behaving Badly,* not only about the institution, but about ourselves.

In short, the Congress this book describes is as full of contradictions as *Congress Behaving Badly* appears to be . . . and it is appropriate. The picture that emerges is that Congress is complicated and contradictory and sometimes in conflict with itself because so is America: complicated and contradictory and often in conflict.

That is the nature of a democracy.

Sunil Ahuja recognizes that the way we elect Congress, the way we draw districts, and (I would add) the number of members we elect have gone largely unchanged during a century of monumental growth, change, and conflict. That was a century whose beginnings were marked by Henry Ford and the Wright Brothers, spanned two World Wars, a fifty-year nuclear standoff, and several trips to the moon. In some ways, it is amazing the place has worked as well as it has for this long using rules and conventions whose roots were grounded in Philadelphia 220 years ago. Maybe it is because a lot of people have wanted it to. Count me among them: to be among those who stand up for the institution and try to make it work.

And then read this book to the end. Do not skip to the last page. It is better if you absorb it all. And if you do, my guess is you will want it to work as much as I do.

Tom Sawyer
Ohio State Representative
Mayor, City of Akron
U.S. Congressman
Member, Ohio State Board of Education
Ohio State Senator

PREFACE

This book is like a documentary. It expresses my point of view, but it is based upon facts. The primary fact is that the U.S. Congress has become a bitter place. The last few decades have seen an enormous rise in hostility and confrontation. Many in the new crop of members, from both sides of the aisle, are intensely partisan in their political orientation, who often engage in acrimonious and uncivil behavior and readily question the motives of their colleagues.

My aim in this book, after identifying the causes and discussing the consequences of partisan and uncivil behavior, is to make a plea for pragmatism and moderation. I suggest a number of reforms, as I believe certain elements of the political system are in need of basic repair. While pragmatism and moderation are labeled the enterprise of the boring by their critics, I believe that in a democracy those are the only productive means to achieving successful ends. Parts of this book will seem harsh on Republicans, as other recent books on this subject have been, but as those works have also suggested, Republicans were in charge when most of the recent partisan warfare occurred. Democrats, though, are no angels in this matter.

I am forever grateful to Bill Binning, my former chair, and to Bob Bolla and Ikram Khawaja, my former deans, for awarding me reassigned time for research to write this book. A special thank you to Hilary Claggett, my former editor at Praeger, for accepting this project, and to Robert Hutchinson for shepherding it to its completion. My thanks also to Christy Anitha for her diligence in editing this manuscript. Finally, my immense thanks to Julia, my wife, for her support. I have enjoyed writing this book for the past few years, and I hope the readers will enjoy reading it.

Sunil Ahuja

CHAPTER 1

THE PROBLEM OF INCIVILITY AND PARTISANSHIP

Men judge by the complexion of the sky
The state and inclination of the day:
So may you by my dull and heavy eye,
My tongue hath but a heavier tale to say.
I play the torturer, by small and small
To lengthen out the worst that must be spoken.

William Shakespeare, *King Richard II*, act 3,
sc. 2, 194–99

If you agree with me on nine out of twelve issues, vote for me.
If you agree with me on twelve out of twelve issues, see a
psychiatrist.

Edward Koch, former mayor of New York

In a National Public Radio broadcast one morning, Cokie Roberts, well-known Washington journalist and daughter of a famous former congressman, said:

> Growing up in Washington in the 1950s, one of my best friends was Libby
> Miller. Her father, Bill Miller, was a Republican congressman from New
> York; my father, Hale Boggs, was a Democratic congressman from New
> Orleans. They each fought their way up the party ladders....These were
> men who played hardball politics, who could take on foes ferociously—
> these men were partisans....Washington was a much less frenzied place in
> those years. When the day's votes ended, congressmen...didn't rush off to
> some fundraiser hosted by a lobbyist. Instead, they gathered in someone's
> office and broke out the bourbon and branch. Most members moved here
> for the session and moved "home," as it was always called, for the recess.
> The ones who "batched it" in the capital expected their colleagues' wives,

regardless of party, to provide dinner on a regular basis. The wives knew each other well. They saw each other at the club for congressional spouses....The wives joined PTAs and ran charitable organizations together....None of that is true today. What changed it? So many things, like the race for money, the weekend rush back to the home district. In the time-honored tradition of running against the institution where they want to serve, congressional candidates assail Washington as an inside-the-Beltway island at best; as a sinful Sodom on the Potomac at worst. So, many families never move here—never run into each other at church, never chaperone dancing school at the Congressional Club. The parties have become more ideologically homogenous, as Southern Democrats either switched parties or lost to Republicans, and Northern and Midwestern Republicans suffered similar fates at the hands of Democrats. Add to that the carefully computerized drawing of congressional districts to create safe seats, and you end up with members who never have to talk to someone who doesn't agree with them, much less listen. And then there's the media. Microphones go to the loudest, most outrageous voice. The boring guy in the middle hardly merits airtime or print inches. And the shrillness of blogs makes anyone who isn't a flamethrower look like a wimp.[1]

In his book *How Congress Works and Why You Should Care*, Lee Hamilton, a former Democratic congressman from Indiana, writes:

One of the more disturbing changes I've witnessed since 1965 has been the decline in civility among members. Certainly the history of Congress has been marked by rough periods, but too often in recent years politics has meant bitter partisan exchanges and mean personal attacks. We have sometimes seen more emphasis on questioning motives than on debating the pros and cons of the issue itself. One member coming off the House floor summed it up simply: "Man, it's rough out there." Spirited debate is appropriate, even healthy, and Congress remains a safe forum in which the conflicts within our society can be aired. But antagonism, incivility, and the tendency to demonize opponents all make it very difficult for members to come together to pass legislation for the good of the country.[2]

In his memoir about government service entitled *Locked in the Cabinet*, Robert Reich, former Secretary of Labor, relays the following story of a meeting in 1994 with Bob Michel, a former Republican congressman from Illinois and House minority leader:

Bob Michel is the House minority leader, the chieftain of the Republican tribe....He has a kindly face topped by a shock of white hair, and speaks in a mellifluous baritone. The overall effect is grandfatherly.

Michel has just announced his decision to retire from the House and not seek another term, and I sense his ambivalence and sadness. He seems less interested in talking about job training than about what he sees happening to the House of Representatives, particularly the Republicans.

"This place used to be very civil," he says, leaning back in his chair. "Republicans and Democrats often saw things differently, of course, but we respected one another. We could work on education and job training, or health care, or welfare, and actually get something done. We respected the *institution*."

"You see that changing?"

"It's becoming a different world up here. That's a big part of why I'm getting out. There's a new breed. They don't care about getting anything done. All they want to do is tear things down. The right wing is gaining ground. It will be our undoing, eventually."

"You mean Gingrich?"

"And his friends." Michel's voice grows softer. "They talk as if they're interested in ideas, in what's good for America. But don't be fooled. They're out to destroy. They'll try to destroy anything that gets in their way, using whatever tactics are available. They don't believe in bipartisanship. I don't really know what they believe in." (emphasis in original)[3]

These episodes paint a not-so-pretty picture of the modern Congress. In the last two decades, the Congress of the United States has become a bitter place of work. Once a collegial institution, it is now a confrontational body. Once an institution where members took pride in friendships and trust, it is now a body where many detest and distrust those on the other side of the aisle. Once an institution held in relatively high esteem by the public, it is now a body with many members who are regarded about as respectfully as used car salesmen, insurance agents, and telemarketers.

The politics of Congress is decidedly too partisan at the moment. An evenly divided nation, where each party claims roughly a third of the country's population, with the remaining third not aligning with either political party, both major parties desperately cling to their base. Both major parties are in effect minority parties. Both sides keep working feverishly to gain some ground in the number of seats in Congress and among voters, and both sides keep thinking that they are losing. In this atmosphere, neither party can afford to lose a single voter, for that would minimize its clout. This configuration is a recipe for extremism, creating an intensely competitive and an extremely tense situation. Both parties resort to constantly looking at their numbers, both in Congress and in the electorate, and take steps accordingly.

In this state, the issues are viewed only through partisan lenses, producing an "anything goes" atmosphere. Whatever works for the party goes. Whatever works to strengthen the influence of one party over the other goes. If one party has to demonize the other side to make itself look better to the voters, that is fine. If one party has to hold off or, worse yet, vote against its own issue so as to not "give" that issue to the other side, such as the Democrats on Medicare or the GOP on balanced budgets, regardless of what happens to millions of affected citizens, that is fine. If the majority party has to keep an issue off the agenda because it is an election year, regardless of its deleterious effects on the people and the nation, that is fine. It all comes down to "positioning" and "strategizing" and "situating" oneself better than the other side. It all comes down to political maneuvering and gamesmanship, where only the bottom line, the "W" (win) counts, and little else matters.

In this state, members hasten to personalize everything. Because the two sides are evenly divided, neither side can have its way. Because neither side can have its way, each side, largely out of sheer frustration, resorts to name-calling and finger-pointing, rather than attempting to understand its opponents and putting things in context. Name-calling begets contempt, contempt begets distrust, and distrust undermines working relationships and friendships across the aisle, and as a result a rational legislative process falls apart.

In this state, a fundamental malfunction occurs in a legislative body, a body that is innately designed for members to work collectively and cooperatively, not individually and independently. The U.S. Congress faces increasingly complex issues and vast numbers of them. Members of Congress face more constraints than ever before in terms of budgets, time, and public opinion. In this situation, working collectively to arrive at public policy solutions acceptable to both sides would be a sensible strategy. But, limited resources make party unity a survival strategy. The social fabric that once bridged this partisan divide no longer exists. Simple "socializing" that once enabled members to have human contacts with each other, producing some affinity for each other by putting politics aside at least after work, no longer exists. Lacking that social glue, each side digs in for a political fight on every major issue.

This state of affairs generates severely negative consequences for both the members and the institution. Constant partisanship is viewed by the public as "bickering" among members, resulting in less popular respect for and confidence in representatives and senators. Moreover, the members' own routine trashing of Congress for partisan reasons diminishes respect for the institution, the very institution in which members earn their living and would do almost anything to win reelections, and one that is a symbol of democracy in the United States and around the world. In addition, constant partisanship and a lack of willingness to compromise significantly hamper the legislative process, leaving major issues unresolved year after year.

Thomas Mann, a noted political scientist at the Brookings Institution, describes the current state of affairs in the following manner:

> Too often in today's politics, battles are waged as a choice between truth and falsehood, not between competing truths. Every fight is regarded as fundamental, with differences unbridgeable. When the central issues of politics involve competing understandings of morality, the ensuing culture wars involve battles between camps that neither understand nor respect each other....One side upholds tradition, religion, the two-parent family, personal responsibility, and hard work; the other, tolerance, openness, diversity, freedom, and creativity. Yet the upholders of tradition are often seen by their foes as bigoted and narrow-minded, repressive and moralistic. The upholders of openness are often seen by their enemies as immoral and irresponsible, libertine and decadent. Such all-out wars over public morality easily spill over into all-out assaults on the moral characters of the individuals who play the central roles in these conflicts. It becomes harder and harder to draw the line between public and private when so much of the political debate is over the public meaning of private moral acts, and the consequences of publicly proclaimed moral codes. If the personal is political, the political becomes very personal. Now, in contemporary politics, this has taken the form of the politics of accusation and moral annihilation. Rather than engage one's adversaries substantively, it becomes easier to undermine him or her personally....We now think first in Congress not of engaging a political adversary in debate, but of filing an ethics charge, or of calling for an independent counsel. That's how we fight our battles today.[4]

This is a sad state in a country with a fully developed democratic system, where politicians are supposed to be mature and people are supposed to understand the democratic principles.

The prevailing political life was also summed up accurately by John McCain, GOP senator from Arizona, in his address to the Republican National Convention in 2000. He said, "Too often those who hold a public trust have failed to set the necessary example. Too often, partisanship seems all consuming. Differences are defined with derision. Too often, we seem to put our personal interests before the national interest, leaving the people's business unattended while we posture, poll and spin."[5]

The public, for its part, clearly seems to dislike constant partisanship and would prefer compromise and moderation from time to time. In an NBC News/Wall Street Journal Poll conducted in 2006, when asked for the reasons of disapproving the job Congress is doing, the top response, at 44 percent, was "tired of Republicans and Democrats fighting." The response after that, at 36 percent, was "nothing gets done on issues important to you."[6] On the other hand, large sums of people prefer bipartisanship. The results of a survey conducted in 2007 by NPR News and the Pew Research Center showed that a solid three-quarters of those polled said "they like political leaders who are willing to compromise, compared with 21 percent who see this as a negative trait." In a show for moderation, nearly two-thirds (62 percent) said they "dislike political leaders who take liberal positions on nearly all issues" and 57 percent said they dislike "political leaders who take conservative positions on nearly all issues." But, by 60 to 34 percent, "more Americans like leaders who take a mix of conservative and liberal positions."[7]

When did this overt bitterness in Congress begin and became a matter of institutional problem? Most observers note the mid-1980s as the starting point. The first beginning mark, in the contemporary Congress, involved a controversial election in 1984 in Indiana's Eighth Congressional District. (This episode is detailed at the beginning of chapter 2.) The second event involves President Ronald Reagan's nomination of Judge Robert Bork to the U.S. Supreme Court in 1987. Since then, nominations, particularly to the High Court, have become extremely contentious. In 1991, partisanship and vitriol surrounded the nomination of Clarence Thomas, tapped by President George H.W. Bush. Nominations to lower federal courts have also created partisan flares. Several of President Bill Clinton's lower court nominees were either denied a hearing or rejected by the Senate Judiciary Committee. Some of President George W. Bush's lower federal court nominees met similar fates.

In their book *The Broken Branch,* Thomas Mann and Norman Ornstein point to 1984 as the starting point of vitriolic behavior in Congress. They write, "[b]y 1984, it was clear that the tension between the two parties had grown to a striking degree. First erupting in mid-year over the special orders that came to be known as 'Camscam,' animosity grew even more rancorous in early and mid-1985 over a disputed congressional election in Indiana."[8] Juliet Eilperin too draws the line at roughly the same time. In her book *Fight Club Politics*, she says: "The past two decades of political polarization—starting with Indiana's Bloody Eighth and Robert Bork's failed Supreme Court nomination, running through the Republican Revolution...throw into question whether House Republicans and Democrats can collaborate for a sustained period of time."[9] Senator Richard Durbin, a Democrat from Illinois and a member of the Senate Judiciary Committee, observed: "Bork's nomination 'set the stage for the current tension in the Senate over judicial nominees.'"[10]

Indeed, the battle over judicial selections has become the latest front in partisan wars in Congress. In years past, in making judicial picks, the ideology of the candidate was considered to be off the table by both the presidents and the Congress. Candidates were selected based upon their education, knowledge, experience, integrity, and so on. But now, ideology has entered into the fray, which means that conservatives do not like liberals simply because they are liberals, and vice versa. The selection of judges based upon ideology makes it largely a "personal" matter for the senators, rather than keeping it at the "professional" level of education, experience, and so forth. Hence, judicial selection has now been "personalized," so that personal dislike by senators has become a point of disqualification rather than whether or not the nominee is reasonable and can be an impartial jurist.

The rancor between the two sides over federal judicial selections rose to unprecedented levels in the fall of 2003. Frustrated by what Republicans called Democrats' unfair and partisan obstruction of GOP nominees, GOP senators launched a nearly 40-hour filibuster, complaining about the unfair treatment of Republican picks by the Democrats. Partisan tempers rose on both sides of the aisle, and Republicans threatened revenge on the next Democratic nominees.[11]

Additionally, nominations for cabinet posts, such as the attorney general, have also become more political. Both of President Clinton's initial picks for the attorney general, Zoe Baird and Kimba Wood, were withdrawn for partisan reasons early in his first term. In 2001, President Bush faced similar contentiousness when he chose former Missouri Senator John Ashcroft to be the attorney general and

Linda Chavez to be the secretary of labor. Chavez was forced to withdraw her name and Ashcroft was confirmed by a narrow vote of 55-45, after a bitter partisan struggle.

The bitter ideological fires are further ignited by the infusion of social issues into the political arena. Historically, social issues rarely entered American politics, with a few possible exceptions, such as the issue of slavery during the nineteenth century. But, led by the Supreme Court's decisions in the 1960s and 1970s on race and abortion, social issues now regularly grace the front page in American politics. These issues are heavily personal and intensely divisive, and politicians routinely play on them to draw lines between the parties. Starting in the late 1980s and thereafter, social issues are increasingly used by both political parties as "wedge" issues to divide the electorate for partisan profit. In the 1988 presidential campaign, the GOP made race an issue to divide the voters. Abortion and immigration were prominent divisive themes abused by both parties in the 1990s. In the 2004 presidential election cycle, the issue of gay marriage became the political football of choice.

Finally, add to this mix the increasingly partisan investigations by members of Congress of presidents of the opposing party. The Democrats pressured for the Iran-Contra probe when Reagan was president. The Republicans pursued President Clinton endlessly from "travelgate" to Whitewater to the Monica Lewinsky affair. And the Democrats called for investigations to find out how much President Bush knew beforehand about the terrorist attacks of September 11, 2001, and whether or not he misled the American public about weapons of mass destruction in Iraq.[12] All these investigations have occurred at an enormous expense to the American people in terms of money and time, and at a cost of diminishing credibility for members of Congress.

The result is a highly charged atmosphere on many issues on Capitol Hill. Members more and more resort to their own camps, socialize only with their own kind, and increase their dislike for the other side and publicly question their motives. This makes the already difficult task of governing nearly impossible.

—————

The 1950s, 1960s, and 1970s were a graceful time in Congress. It was a time when congressmen and women got along with each other. Despite their political differences, members respected and trusted those on the other side of the aisle. During this time, members appear to have kept personal issues out of politics. Where members disagreed, it was because of partisan or ideological reasons. The differences were not reduced to personal insults or finger-pointing.

That sense of professionalism and warmth has been lost on the Hill. In the early 1960s, Congressman Clem Miller, Democrat of California, could describe Congress as follows: "One's overwhelming first impression as a member of Congress is the aura of friendliness that surrounds the life of a congressman. No wonder that 'few die and none resign.' Almost everyone is unfailingly polite and courteous. Window washers, clerks, senators—it cuts all ways. We live in a cocoon of good feeling."[13] By contrast, consider the following remarks made some twenty years later, in the early 1980s, by Senator Joseph Biden, Democrat of Delaware:

> There's much less civility than when I came here ten years ago. There aren't as many nice people as there were before....Ten years ago you didn't have people calling each other sons of bitches and vowing to get at each other. The first few years, there was only one person who, when he gave me his word, I had to go back to the office to write it down. Now there's two dozen of them. As you break down the social amenities one by one, it starts expanding geometrically. Ultimately you don't have any social control....We end up with 100 Proxmires here. One...makes a real contribution. All you need is 30 of them to guarantee that the place doesn't work.[14]

The two statements represent a dramatic contrast in the institution. The former was a collegial body, a productive institution, and a pleasant place of work. The latter has become a mean-spirited body, an increasingly unpleasant place of work, where more and more reasonable and moderate members choose to voluntarily retire and resign rather than deal with the partisan pettiness on the Hill.

From a broader perspective, the Congress has altered dramatically in recent decades. Mann and Ornstein, in a section in *The Broken Branch* called "Roots of the Problem," describe the causes in the following fashion: "This is an era characterized by strong and ideologically polarized parties competing from positions of rough parity. These features of the party system are evident among elected officials in government and in the electorate....Fewer states are up for grabs in presidential elections and the number of competitive contests for the Senate and especially for the House has dropped markedly....The roots of this distinctly partisan era are deep and complex." They cite the breakup of the New Deal coalition, the cultural and civil rights struggles of the 1960s, the Voting Rights Act of 1965, the Vietnam conflict, the Supreme Court's *Roe v. Wade* decision in 1973, and the economic and national security battles of the 1980s and the 1990s. They continue:

> As these developments played out over time, party platforms grew more distinctive, those recruited to Congress became more ideologically in tune with their fellow partisans, and voters increasingly sorted themselves into the two parties based on their ideological views. At the same time, voters were making residential decisions that reinforced the ideological sorting already under way....Both bipartisan and partisan gerrymanders contributed further to these effects. And they were reinforced by interest groups that increasingly aligned themselves with one party or the other and radio and cable news and talk shows that pitched to distinctive partisan and ideological audiences....But politicians are not merely waifs amid forces. They make choices about how to organize and run their institution and how to conduct themselves personally, albeit choices constrained by the external environment and the incentives it creates. In recent decades, leaders and members of Congress acted in ways that exacerbated the partisan polarization and intensified the forces leading to institutional decline.[15]

A little earlier in the book, Mann and Ornstein state that "[t]his deeply partisan era was also shaped by the changing nature of individuals coming into the elective arena, characterized by fewer politicians—a term we view with respect, not disdain—who care about compromise, product, and institutional health and more individual activists, ideologues, and entrepreneurs interested in purity and personal advancement."[16]

Many others also lament the current state of affairs. Referring to the changes in the political environment from the 1960s to the present, Joe Klein, in his book *Politics Lost*, writes: "Suddenly, politicians were able to use televised advertising to communicate in a more powerful and intimate (and negative) way than ever before—and suddenly politicians had to raise vast sums of money to pay for those ads. The hours they had spent studying issues, chatting with colleagues, or napping in the past were now devoted to working the phones and trolling for dollars." In this way, "[t]he need for money empowered the special interests of left and right: they provided the bulk of campaign contributions and campaign workers."[17]

Additionally, Bill Keller, writing for the *New York Times,* describes the Congress of then and the Congress of now in the following terms:

> there was a time when the U.S. Congress was an estimable branch of the American government. It was a place where people took lawmaking almost as seriously as winning elections, where strong views were tempered in the interest of solving problems. There was a prevailing aura of good will that reflected the well-meaning homeyness of America. Sometimes memorable and illuminating debates took place.... Now ... it is a collection of spineless led by the cynical, constantly lap-dancing for special-interest cash to finance the permanent campaign, deadlocked not over high principles but over petty partisan advantage and ... incapable of mounting a debate worthy of a junior high school. It makes you heart-sore for the state of democracy.... The reasons for this depressing dysfunction are complicated and cultural. The roughly 50-50 split in Congress raises the stakes and turns every contest into Antietam. The perfection of big-money, sound-bite, attack-ad campaigning has made it harder to defend a thoughtful, principled vote. Lawmakers don't know each other, since they're always home campaigning, so they feel freer to demonize one another.[18]

The changes in Congress noted in these passages reflect the sadness, at best, that many observers have, and disgust, at worst, that many have, for contemporary American politics generally.

The reasons for this sad state of affairs in Congress outlined in the above quotes and discussed at some length later in this chapter are analyzed fully later in this book. One factor, one that could very well be defined as either the cause or the effect of the shift from civility and bipartisanship to a lack of them, has been the change in the "type" of members serving in Congress over the last twenty or so years. Upon the retirements of Congressman Bill Archer, Republican of Texas, and Senator Daniel Patrick Moynihan, Democrat of New York, the *Dallas Morning News* led an editorial with the following: "When Bill Archer and Daniel Patrick Moynihan came to Congress in the 1970s, politics was practiced differently. Leaders had sharp, pointed disagreements. But blood rarely flowed in the halls.... That equation has changed. Today, both houses of Congress have many fierce believers who fail to separate ideas from individuals. They prefer to turn their philosophical opponents into demons and escalate political disagreements into personal antagonisms."[19] It is widely believed that many of the members of the 1950s, 1960s, and 1970s were pragmatic and appreciated the legislative process. Many of today's members are exactly the opposite.

Indeed, the last two decades have witnessed the retirements of many moderate members of Congress. The conciliatory members on both sides of the aisle voluntarily departed, unable to work in an increasingly unpleasant institution. Their mark was not their partisanship, for they hailed from both parties, but rather their respect and trust for those on the other side despite their ideological differences. The following list is by no means all-inclusive, but a few memorable names come to mind. In addition to Archer and Moynihan, consider the departures of Tom Foley, former Democratic Speaker from Washington (defeated in his reelection), Lee Hamilton, Democrat of Indiana, Sam Nunn, Democrat of Georgia, Warren Rudman, Republican of New Hampshire, Mark Hatfield, Republican of Oregon, John Chafee, Republican of Rhode Island, William Cohen, Republican of Maine, and John Breaux, Democrat of Louisiana, among others.[20]

The confrontational members have replaced the conciliatory ones. The newer members are distrustful of the other side. They show no respect, and refuse to socialize with their opponents. Indeed, the fundamental crux of the problem is that the new members not only think that the other side is wrong, but rather that it is evil. Many of these are from the South, and many of these were part of the Republican revolution that swept through Capitol Hill in 1994. Here also many names come to mind, but again this list is not fully inclusive. This camp includes Newt Gingrich, former Republican Speaker of the House from Georgia, Tom DeLay, Republican of Texas, Bob Livingston, Republican of Louisiana, Bob Barr, Republican of Georgia, Bob Dornan, Republican of California, Bob Walker, Republican of Pennsylvania, Nancy Pelosi, Democrat of California, David Bonior, Democrat of Michigan, Charles Schumer, Democrat of New York, Rick Santorum, Republican of Pennsylvania, Jeff Sessions, Republican of Alabama, and Mitch McConnell, Republican of Kentucky, among others.[21]

It is important to note that the increased animus and blatant partisanship in the present Congress did not begin with the Republican revolution of 1994, having established earlier in this chapter as the mid-1980s being the starting point. The new breed of Republicans that swept the Hill in 1994, however, did significantly exaggerate the trends toward animus and partisanship. As Mann and Ornstein write, "[c]racks in the institution began to show in the 1980s and early 1990s, during the last decade of the forty-year hegemony of Democrats in the

House."[22] Eilperin writes, "[a]fter enjoying decades of unrivaled control, Democrats became increasingly dictatorial in the 1980s." During that time, Democratic leaders, afraid of losing power, "started cracking down on House Republicans even when it did not make the difference between winning or losing a vote. They limited opportunities for debate, publicly mocked members of the minority, and frequently denied Republicans the chance to make their mark on legislation." However, after the GOP took over in 1994, she adds, "I saw firsthand how Republican revolutionaries worked to solidify their control and dismantle institutions that promoted compromise, even as they took steps to reform Congress. And I witnessed how Democrats responded in kind, becoming more partisan and wedded to interest groups that drove the two parties further apart."[23]

The space between the two camps, between Democrats and Republicans and between "new" and "old" style members, is so great that each thinks of the other as some total strangers from a foreign land. As Eilperin writes:

> it is hard to exaggerate how much House Republicans and Democrats dislike each other these days. The much-discussed red state-blue state divide captures the duality, but not the animus, of this relationship. They speak about their opponents as if they hail from a distant land with strange customs, all of which are twisted. Republicans see members of the minority [as the House Democrats were in 2006] as a bunch of sore losers who assail them on procedural grounds because they lack a compelling vision of how to rule the country. Democrats view the GOP majority [as the House Republicans were in 2006] as a ruthless band that will do anything to maintain its power. When asked to describe each other..., House members used words like "control freak," "childish," "asinine," and "whiners."[24]

Quoting Dave Barry, James Q. Wilson conveys the differences between these two camps in the following stark and humorous terms: "residents of Red states are 'ignorant, racist, fascist, knuckle-dragging, Nascar-obsessed, cousin-marrying, road-kill-eating, tobacco-juice-dribbling, gun-fondling, religious fanatic rednecks,' while Blue-state residents are 'godless, unpatriotic, pierced-nose Volvo-driving, France-loving, leftwing Communist, latte-sucking, tofu-chomping, holistic-wacko neurotic, vegan, weenie perverts.'"[25]

In addition to the lack of civility, a vital ingredient missing in the new members is an appreciation for bipartisanship. Somehow, "compromise," "bargain," and "deal-making" are dirty words to many of the new breed. Indeed, compromise and bargaining are essential to the legislative process. The newer members must heed the saying attributed to Sam Rayburn, the former Democratic Speaker of the House from Texas, "to get along, you have to go along."

To a considerable extent, the decline in civility and rise in partisanship are consequences of the demise of norms in Congress. The glue that held members together despite their political differences in the 1950s, 1960s, and 1970s was a set of folkways. Political scientist Donald Matthews identified six of these unwritten rules of behavior: apprenticeship, courtesy, reciprocity, specialization, legislative work, and institutional patriotism.[26] Of these, courtesy, reciprocity, and institutional patriotism are at the heart of the problems of incivility, partisanship, and lack of respect for the institution. There has been significant evidence over the last two decades that these norms have weakened.[27] Members are now less courteous toward each other, and do not trust each other's word. Members of different ideological stripes no longer socialize with each other. Their staffs have few interactions, limited only to congressional work. The new members show total disregard for the institution, the very institution in which they serve and which is a symbol of democracy the world over.

Political scientist Hugh Heclo argues that increased levels of incivility and partisanship have occurred due to the emergence of the "permanent campaign," where there is no distinction between governing and campaigning and the focus tends to be on those elements that build a politician's image and sustain his or her popularity. Heclo notes six factors that have contributed to the permanent campaign in the last few decades. These include the decline of political parties, the growth of interest groups, the creation of new communications technologies, the introduction of new political technologies, the increased need for money in politics, and the higher levels of stakes in an activist government.[28] These factors have created a free-for-all, where parties no longer provide the discipline and interest groups, consultants, pollsters, media and image experts, and money control the candidates and ultimately the political system.

Dealing specifically with an increased lack of civility, political scientist Eric Uslaner suggests five factors that have contributed to the decline of comity in Congress. He notes that the congressional reforms of the 1970s which opened up the decision-making process on Capitol Hill, the increasingly divided control of Congress and the presidency which heightens partisanship, the rise of the media which allows members to play to the camera, the changes in membership in the 1970s that discarded the norms because they did not work to their advantage, and the explosion of self-serving interest groups have each participated in increasing the level of vitriol on Capitol Hill.[29] These factors have also contributed to a free-for-all environment, where members are interested first and foremost in their personal gain, even if it comes at the cost of minimizing the institution and being uncivil.

Finally, Dan Miller, former Republican congressman from Florida, noted six variables that have contributed to the decline of civility. They are redistricting, which has produced an overwhelming majority of safe seats for both parties; the goal of the minority to become the majority (for both parties), an environment that tolerates tearing down the other side; the rise of C-SPAN and the 24-hour cable news media; a realignment in the parties' leadership, where the leaders of both parties are far more ideological than they used to be and refuse to compromise; the lack of social interaction among members; and the contentiousness of issues, particularly the social issues.[30] Each of these factors, argues Miller, add fuel to the fire on Capitol Hill.

The result of all these developments is that we are now in a state where personal or partisan victories are the be-all and end-all of politics. Here, nothing of substance gets done.

What does civility mean? Lee Hamilton defines it as follows: "Simply put, it means that legislators respect the rights and dignity of others. It does not mean that they need to agree with one another— far from it. Rather, treating one another civilly is how people who don't agree still manage to weigh issues carefully and find common ground."[31]

Likewise, to Christopher Darr, based upon other studies, "civil language is respectful of others, both personally and ideologically, where other points of view are acknowledged as legitimate, even if the parties involved disagree. Civil language does not insult or berate; it is courteous and respectful. It may be critical, but not in ways that discourage productive debate by resorting to personal or hostile attacks."[32]

Kathleen Hall Jamieson, in her study of civility in the House, observes that "comity is based on the norm of reciprocal courtesy and presupposes that the differences between members and parties are philosophical not personal, that parties to a debate are entitled to the presumption that their views are legitimate even if not correct, and that those on all sides are persons of good will and integrity motivated by conviction." She adds, "strong partisanship and civility are not mutually exclusive. Pleas for civility are not calls for blurring partisan differences."[33]

Also, to Dr. Rick Warren, famed pastor and author of the best-selling book, *The Purpose Driven Life,* "civility means I'm going to treat you with respect, even if I totally disagree with you." He continues, "there was civil discussion in our society for many years, but it has become so polarized, so rude, and I honestly think people are tired of it. And we need to get back to the idea of we treat each other with respect, we come to the table, we're not disagreeing—we're not downplaying our differences." As for the reasons, he says that "[t]here are legitimate differences and there is no mainstream culture in America. We are many streams. And we are a pluralistic culture. But we have to treat each other with respect and civility."[34]

Why does civility matter? According to the authors of an editorial in the *Des Moines Register,* civility matters "[b]ecause civility, common courtesy, good manners, respect—call it what you will—is the lubricant that prevents the machinery of democracy from rattling apart." The editorial continues, "[m]ore important, civility keeps the door open for compromise and conciliation. On a personal and practical level, members who are on opposite sides on one piece of legislation might be on the same side on the next bill. If you insult a colleague during one debate, you might lose his or her vote when you need it on the next bill. It is a wise lawmaker who remains civil and cultivates friendships across the aisle." The editorial concludes with the following: "Little wonder that civility is slipping away. The fine art of governing has given way to the partisan imperative of winning. Where winning is everything in athletics, sportsmanship dies. Where winning is everything in politics, civility dies."[35]

For Uslaner, "[c]ivil discourse is a sign of trust, harsh rhetoric of distrust. And trust in others is the glue that holds a society together and makes it possible to reach accommodations....Civility takes the rough edges off political and social life. Courtesy makes it easier for strangers and even adversaries to reason together—and to forge compromises. Strong partisans can argue their cases with both passion and grace. Neither side will convert the other, but they may see points of compromise that each would prefer to a stalemate."[36]

Elsewhere, Uslaner notes, ''[c]ivility alone…isn't worth a warm bucket of spit. Civility matters because it is part of comity, a more general syndrome of treating others with respect both in language and in deed.''[37]

At a simple level, to be civil is to be nice. But civility has greater claims than simply being nice. Civility is about having a high regard for human beings, and especially for people that one regularly deals with. Civility is about listening to others, and especially those who have different ideas and perspectives. And civility is about trusting one's colleagues, even those who are of different ideological or partisan persuasions. In other words, civility recognizes and understands disagreements but not disagreeableness.

In political and institutional settings, civility is the grease that lubricates the functioning of a political system, especially the American system that is based upon separation of powers and checks and balances. The Constitution separates the institutions; the political parties separate the individuals. The federal structure provides yet another separation, and the nation's vast diversity in races, regions, religions, and so on adds a variety of other layers to the mix. An unwillingness to be civil and to work with the other side in such a system only aggravates the situation.

Moreover, the lack of civility and partisanship has major implications for a democratic system. The very essence of democracy is that people voice their concerns on matters affecting the state. Quite naturally, everyone will not have the same voices and neither can everyone be forced to have the same voices. For if that were the case, we would be living in an autocratic or a totalitarian state. Democracy requires, indeed even encourages, differences of opinions. The idea in a democratic system is that we all air our opinions in the public square and we hash out our differences through debate and dialogue. In this situation, we must inevitably settle on the solutions that are acceptable to a broad spectrum of people, representing all wings of the debate. As such, moderation wins and extremism loses.

The problem with incivility and partisanship is that it chokes off open dialogue, it minimizes human contact with those with whom we disagree, it limits our ability to understand the differences of opinions, and it engenders distrust of the other side. In such an environment, what has come to transpire in American politics is that institutions make rules because they can, majorities make policies because they can, and public officials abuse each other and institutions because they can. Democrats make the choices that they make because they have the votes and could care less about the Republicans; Republicans select the options that they select because they have the numbers and could care less about the Democrats.

Thus, each side is preoccupied with defeating the other side, almost at any cost. Each side is predisposed to seeing the other side as evil. No one can claim real accomplishments in this situation, and the concerns of the people go unaddressed or remain indefinitely postponed.

An important caveat needs mention. Popular history holds that the lack of civility in Congress is nothing new. When this question comes up, students of history routinely cite cases from the nineteenth century. In early nineteenth century, Matthew Lyon of Kentucky spat at Roger Griswold of Connecticut, for which Griswold beat Lyon with a walking stick. In 1845, Edward Black of Georgia beat Joshua Giddings of Ohio with a cane, and in 1851 Representative Preston Brooks of South Carolina walked into the Senate and beat Senator Charles Sumner of Massachusetts with a cane. John Randolph of Virginia had hunting dogs on the floor. Pistols and fisticuffs often came out in these brawls.[38] "These were not pleasant days," writes Thomas B. Reed. "Men were not nice in their treatment of each other."[39]

These events of incivility, though, were much rarer than the ones we see now. Yes, an occasional caning or tongue-lashing did occur. But today, incivility is a common phenomenon, almost a daily occurrence. Admittedly, members no longer resort to physical abuse, but the number of verbal instances of incivility abound these days. Plus, one must remember that those days were in the midst of a civil war, necessarily producing heated tempers on the many issues of the day. We are not now. As Mann and Ornstein state, "the problems now are different and worrisome. The frontier atmosphere that characterized Congress through much of our early history occurred during a time when Congress convened almost part time and when the role of the federal government was much more limited. There was no mass mobilization, no mass media, no twenty-four-hour cable news." Now, they say, "Congress is much larger, more potent, and part of a federal government with remarkable scope and sweep. Each of its actions or inactions has more consequences."[40]

The contemporary uncivil and partisan condition stands in stark contrast to the collegial days of the 1950s, 1960s, and 1970s. There is no doubt that the period following World War II in Congress was more civil and less partisan than it is now. One need only notice the aforementioned statements by former Congressman Miller and Senator

Biden on this point and other evidence presented later in this book. It is in this context, the post–World War II era, where the evidence in this book is analyzed.

One other important caveat. It is a fact that not all contemporary members of Congress are uncivil or partisan, and that not all contemporary members think of the other side as evil. But enough do, and more and more of them do, so that the animus continues to spread. It takes only a few bad members, says Senator Biden, to ensure that the proper functioning of Congress comes to a grinding halt. As the saying goes, it takes only one rotten apple to spoil the cart.

—————

A number of studies have emerged on this subject. Several sole-authored and edited books have examined various strands of the debate surrounding the rise in partisanship and the decline in civility in Congress.[41] These books, however, have several shortcomings, in some cases through no fault of the authors. Uslaner's book is now somewhat dated, particularly given the increased partisanship and incivility since 1993. The others are collected volumes that focus only on the U.S. Senate. Moreover, these books, as leading sources in this area, and other smaller works on the topic, offer no recommendations intended to reduce intense divisiveness. These books are good analyses of the issue, but offer little in the way of solutions. My purpose herein is to comprehensively examine the issues of partisanship and incivility and to speak to a broad audience about the importance of getting along.

A couple of volumes already cited in this book, Mann and Ornstein's *The Broken Branch* and Eilperin's *Fight Club Politics*, are commendable broad analyses of the topic and do offer some solutions. But even here, Mann and Ornstein's book focuses a lot on the rules and procedures of the House and Eilperin's book focuses a lot on the question of redistricting as the basis of partisanship and vitriol in the House.

In this book, I argue that the lack of comity and the employment of raw partisanship for the purpose of political gain are incompatible with democratic systems. I then note the examples of increased incivility in Congress. In the next chapter, I identify the changes in membership of the House and Senate over the postwar years, and distinguish between the "old style" and the "new style" member. I then fully delve into the causes of uncivil debate and partisanship on the Hill. Next, I show a major consequence of incivility and partisan behavior, the decline in public confidence and support for members and the institution. This is a key finding that has thus far not been discussed elsewhere. I then discuss the consequences of uncivil and partisan behavior on the legislative process. I conclude with some solutions designed to curb partisan warfare and make an exhortation for getting along with the other side.

I wish to make a plea for pragmatism in this book. Thus, this book is partly a polemic. This book is intended to appeal to members of Congress to stop the spread of venomous behavior for personal or partisan gain. It is written to urge the restoration of civility, bipartisanship, and moderation. The arguments and evidence presented in this book show that getting personal and being partisan corrode public confidence and respect not only for the members but for the institution as well. This book shows that name-calling and deriding others for differences of opinion do not go hand-in-hand with democratic principles and with the proper functioning of representative assemblies. All told, this book is intended to convey that moderation is the key to real success.

The primary method employed in this book is historical research. I study the questions and concerns raised above by examining legislators' speeches, statements, and observations about their colleagues and the institution. These statements and observations were researched through a variety of sources, such as the *Congressional Record,* members' interviews with the media, and press releases. In addition, research and writings by observers of Congress, both academics and journalists, on this topic were also studied. Data on members' party unity and ideology, on the public's views of members and the institution, and on the open and restrictive rules and cloture votes were gathered through a collection of public sources. The period under analysis in this book is the postwar years.

I have written this book not so much for my academic brethren, but for a general audience, for anyone who loves to read, for anyone interested in American politics, for anyone who cares about the state of our democracy. I hope the general reader, and my academic colleagues as well, will take away a good bit from this book.

CHAPTER 2

THE CAPITOL HILL
JUNIOR HIGH SCHOOL

If you prick us, do we not bleed?
if you tickle us, do we not laugh?
if you poison us, do we not die?
and if you wrong us, shall we not revenge?

William Shakespeare, *The Merchant of Venice*,
act 3, sc. 1, 66–69

I would say I'd like to see a culture of civility. Our civilization
is becoming less civil. It's just gotten quite rude. And you don't
have a right to demonize somebody just because they're
different.

Pastor Rick Warren

In an article in the *Chautauquan Daily*, William Clinger, a former
Republican congressman from Pennsylvania who served in the House
from 1978 to 1996, writes:

> During the eighteen years I served in the House...I observed a disturbing
> coarsening in the quality of public debate. In the late '70s and early '80s
> there was a spirit of collegiality and civility...that is almost entirely lacking
> today....Debate on controversial issues was often heated and partisan
> 25 years ago but rarely if ever personal. A member could seriously disagree
> with a colleague's opinion while respecting his right to hold it. The level to
> which the House has sunk in recent years is epitomized by an exchange...
> on the floor during my last year in Congress—1996. The subject of the
> debate was abortion—which it too often was and is—and a member was
> citing statistics and evidence which he said supported his position when
> another member with a contrary view took the floor to angrily declare
> "The gentlemen from California is a liar." Disagreeing with a colleague's
> position is one thing; calling him a liar is quite another. It is the antithesis
> of reasoned debate and reduces a hopefully enlightening discussion to

personal vituperation. One of the more arcane motions that may be offered in the House...is a motion to "take down the words" of a member who has allegedly impugned the integrity of a fellow member. If the parliamentarian rules in favor of the motion, it means that the offensive words are stricken from the official record of the day's proceedings. In my first five years in Congress the motion was invoked only twice. In my last five, barely a week went by when someone wasn't demanding that a member's words "be taken down."[1]

In an online discussion about partisanship and incivility in government, former Senator David Pryor, a Democrat from Arkansas, noted the following:

> I think that it is the civility that worries me so much more than the rising statistics of partisanship votes in the past twenty or thirty years in the House and Senate....They're still—most of the Congress are very civilized people, and they want to conduct their businesses in a civilized way. But 30 years ago we would never think of going into a state and campaigning against one of our colleagues, for example, who's our seat mate maybe at the lunch counter or down in the Senate dining room. We would never think about going out and raising money against one of our colleagues, or, if we did, we would certainly call 'em on the phone and say, hey, Jack, I'm coming to your state this weekend; I'm not going to say anything rough about you; I know you will know that I'm your friend. We just don't seem to have that same thing.[2]

That was then. Now, it is quite different. Modern congressional life is not a pleasant endeavor. It is nasty, vindictive, and personal. It is mean and petty. It is an environment that is much more likely to be witnessed in the playgrounds of junior high schools across the nation than it should be seen on the floors of the most esteemed legislative body in the world. The nastiness is ever-present, and neither party has a monopoly on it. It is a decease that afflicts members on both sides of the aisle. Indeed, as they take turns, each side gets meaner than the other, uglier than the previous stab, as if to do one-better than before.

In this chapter, my goal is to describe to the readers the many examples of increased incivility in Congress. I shall show the increasing vindictiveness in the branch of government at the center of the nation's capital, and reveal how pervasive the bitterness has become. There is more name-calling and finger-pointing than ever before, the discussion rapidly gets undignified and personal than ever before, and the members are ready at their feet to question each other's motives and indeed pledge revenge more than ever before.

Such is the sad state of contemporary legislative life on the Hill. As noted in chapter 1 and in the above quote by Senator Pryor, it is important to keep in mind that there still are many members of Congress who conduct their business in a civil and bipartisan fashion. But, as he also indicates, there are more and more members who readily engage in acrimonious behavior, who question their colleagues' motives, and who are ready to trash their colleagues. The examples in this chapter cover about the last quarter century of congressional politics.

———◆———

In contemporary memory, from the mid-1980s, marking the beginnings of the current streak of extended uncivil behavior in Congress, there is an episode that occurred on May 8, 1984. On that day, Congressman Newt Gingrich, later to be speaker of the House, placed into the *Congressional Record* a report that criticized the foreign policy record of dozens of House Democrats. About a week later, in response, Tip O'Neill, then Speaker of the House, criticized Gingrich for attacking the "Americanism" of these Democrats and charged that the former Georgia congressman's behavior was "the lowest thing that I have ever seen in my 32 years in Congress." This infuriated some Republicans. In reply, Representative Trent Lott, Republican from Mississippi and then the House minority whip, launched a protest and demanded that the speaker's words be taken down. They were, and O'Neill was rebuked.[3]

The episode that is frequently touted as the beginning point in the decline of civility in Congress took place in the aftermath of the 1984 congressional elections. In this case, a dispute arose over a contested election in Indiana. The race between Frank McCloskey, the incumbent Democrat representing the Eighth District, and Richard D. McIntyre, his Republican challenger, turned out to be extremely close. On election night, McCloskey appeared to have carried the seat by 72 votes. However, a House-sponsored recount put McCloskey ahead by 4 votes out of the 230,000 cast, while two state recounts put McIntyre ahead by 34 and 418 votes. The House Democrats, in charge at the time as the majority, accepted the results of the House-sponsored recount, and decided to award the seat to their own, Democrat McCloskey.

This incident produced an outrage among the minority Republicans, whose leader, Michel, led a protest against the House Democrats.

The Republicans, who felt cheated out of a seat, launched "a campaign of legislative harassment" against the Democrats by tying up the House floor for the next several days on procedural matters. Jack Kemp, then a Republican congressman from New York, said "[t]he delaying tactics are designed to raise the consciousness of the Democrats." Other Republicans took to the Capitol steps and chanted the famous civil rights slogan, "We Shall Overcome."[4] Bob Dornan, a California GOP congressman known for his firebrand rhetoric, called awarding the seat to McCloskey instead of McIntyre, a "rape," whereas Michel said it was a sign of "autocratic rule."[5]

David Rapp, the editor of the *Congressional Quarterly Weekly Reports*, observes that "seating McCloskey over McIntyre was a power play, pure and simple. The Democrats put him in the seat because they could." The McCloskey seat had absolutely no impact on Democratic control of the House, since they already held a 252-182 majority. It was all about power. Even moderate Republicans, as Bill Thomas of California was then, called the act to seat McCloskey as "nothing short of rape." Writes Rapp, "the McCloskey-McIntyre imbroglio became an empowering moment for Thomas and his fellow Republicans. Though it would take nine more years for the GOP to climb into power in the House, their back bench 'bomb throwers'—Robert Walker, Newt Gingrich, and Dick Armey—became the voice of the party in the intervening years, ultimately replacing the moderating influences of Bob Michel [and others]."[6]

The acrimony between the two parties on Capitol Hill has accelerated since then. In 1985, an open barroom-style brawl occurred between Congressman Thomas Downey, Democrat from New York, and Dornan, the California Republican. In this instance, Dornan grabbed Downey by his tie and, in his usual inflammatory style, confronted him and other Democrats of not being tough on national security. Congressman Ted Weiss, Democrat from New York, had offered an amendment to the 1986 defense bill, one designed to eliminate funds for the Trident II D5 nuclear missile. In the House floor debate on the amendment, several moderate and liberal Democrats spoke in favor of it. However, Dornan, an ultra-hawk, opposed the amendment and lashed out at some Democrats for supporting it. He attacked then-Representative Barbara Boxer, a Democrat from California, calling her "the gentlelady from Babylon by the Bay," referring to San Francisco. He fired off at then-Representative Les AuCoin, Democrat from Oregon, yelling, "You're for absolutely nothing. You voted for nothing in your life for defense. You sit up here with your mouth dripping spleen and bile." Indeed, Dornan went even further, charging all those without military service, "Those of you that have no military record are the most offensive ones of all." AuCoin objected to these remarks, demanding that Dornan should be ruled out of order and lose his speaking rights for the rest of the day. After this scene, some of his GOP colleagues took Dornan aside, and, after calming down a bit, he apologized for his outburst.[7]

The episodes of this sort have continued unabatedly since then. Sometimes they occur even between members of the same party. In one infamous case, Bob Michel, the moderate GOP leader, and Jack Kemp, the conservative, got into a row over the U.S. policy toward the Contras in Nicaragua. Kemp accused his leader of not working hard enough to line up votes for aid to the Contras. In a pointed departure from his style of doing business, Michel publicly blasted Kemp, then the Republican caucus chairman. In an interview with *Roll Call*, a Capitol Hill newspaper, Michel said, "There's an awful lot of difference [between] standing on the sidelines talking about the issue and working the issue here with the votes you got. Jack Kemp does not have that experience of working an issue."[8]

Newt Gingrich, for his part, continued the downward slide on the slippery slope of incivility. One of his famous clashes of acrimony occurred with Jim Wright. In 1988, the future speaker of the House filed ethics complaints against Congressman Wright, then the Democratic speaker of the House, which led to a highly partisan confrontation and ultimately to Wright's resignation from the House. Gingrich accused Wright of violating the House rules on various occasions, particularly involving a book deal that Wright had signed. In his remarks prior to his resignation, Wright said, "[a]ll of us, in both political parties, must resolve to bring this period of mindless cannibalism to an end." To which Michel, the minority leader, replied, "[n]ow it's a catchy phrase, but the distinguished members of the ethics committee...are neither mindless nor cannibals. I am all for putting an end to bitterness...but we don't do so by sweeping things under the rug."[9]

And in yet another case, former Congressman Henry Hyde, Republican of Illinois, normally among the least acrimonious members of the House, almost broke into a fistfight with Massachusetts Democrat Barney Frank. Hyde became furious at a mocking speech by Frank alleging Michel, the Republican leader, of changing his positions on a budget resolution. In defending Michel, Hyde chided Frank for mischaracterizing the Republican leader's original speech.

Frank, retorted Hyde, was not on the House floor when Michel stated his positions on the resolution, but was perhaps in the House gym, "doing whatever he does when he's in the gymnasium." That comment referred back to an earlier accusation against Frank that he had had sex with a prostitute in the House gym. The accusation was disproven as a result of an inquiry by the House Ethics Committee. After reconsidering his remark, Hyde apologized, and asked that his comment be removed from the record. As this skirmish was playing out, Representative Craig Washington, Democrat from Texas, and Bob Walker, former Republican congressman from Pennsylvania, "almost squared off in an aisle as Washington rushed to the GOP side to talk privately with Hyde," apparently about Hyde's comment concerning Frank.[10]

The Senate, of course, is not immune from such acrimoniousness. Senators, too, know how to get dirty. John Heinz, the former GOP senator from Pennsylvania, made a provocative statement on the Senate floor one day, to which Lowell Weicker, the former liberal GOP senator from Connecticut, responded: "[a]nyone who would make such a statement is either devious or an idiot. The gentleman from Pennsylvania qualifies on both counts."[11] These words were taken down and never made it into the *Congressional Record*. In 1983, in a dispute over Central America between Barry Goldwater, former Republican senator from Arizona, and Christopher Dodd, Democrat from Connecticut, Goldwater publicly lashed out a personal attack against Dodd, saying, "I served with Dodd's father and I have tremendous respect for his father. I think one of Chris' main troubles is that he's trying to live up to his old man and he can't do it. And the evidence is that the two men who called for the session [for the dispute] made utter fools of themselves with the information they thought they had."[12] In another quarrel, this time between Mark Andrews, former GOP senator from North Dakota, and Jesse Helms, former GOP senator from North Carolina, Andrews referred to Helms and those on the Senate Agriculture Committee who supported his policies as "Jesse and his pack of thieves."[13]

Indeed, on the Senate side, former Senate Republican Bob Dole became remarkably famous for getting into quarrels with his colleagues, particularly those on the other side of the aisle.[14] In 1989, in a heated exchange with former Senator Ernest Hollings, Democrat of South Carolina, Dole seemed to elicit an old-fashioned brawl: "I say to my friend from South Carolina, I will be glad to discuss this with him privately, or maybe he wants to go out and make that statement when not protected by speaking from the Senate floor."[15]

As the minority leader, Dole would repeatedly get into arguments with former Senate Democratic leader George Mitchell of Maine. In the summer of 1990, the talk between the two leaders became particularly heated over a civil rights bill. The Democrats wanted the measure, but the Republicans, including then President George H. W. Bush, opposed it. Each side accused the other of playing politics with the legislation. The unified Democratic majority, however, aided by some breakaway Republicans, invoked cloture on the measure over the GOP objections, leading to the passage of the bill. But the Democratic strong-arm tactics employed in invoking cloture infuriated Dole. He accused Mitchell of "gagging" the Republican minority and treating them "like a bunch of bums." Said Senator Thad Cochran, Republican of Mississippi, on the less-than-friendly interactions between the two sides: "[t]he train hasn't wrecked, but it sure is rocking on the tracks." Jack Danforth, former Republican senator from Missouri, said, "I think it actually helped to let off steam." The usually staid David Boren, then a Democratic senator from Oklahoma, noted, "I don't think this left any of us with a good taste in our mouths."[16]

In the House in particular, 1995 was a banner year for incivility. Those were the heady days for the Republicans, since they had just regained majority after forty years in the condemned minority. For the Democrats, there was a lot of getting used to being in the minority, after forty years of enjoying the fruits of the majority status. So, tempers were running high for members of both parties. Guy Gugliotta, writing for the *Washington Post*, reports a number of uncivil cases in that year. In a couple of incidents, showing their usual dislike of President Clinton, members of the GOP fired off at the former president. Dornan, the former California Republican, accused Clinton of treason, and was thrown off the House floor for the rest of the day. In another case, former Congressman John Mica, a Florida Republican, characterized Clinton as a "little bugger," a remark that led to his words being taken down from the House record. On the other hand, many Democrats disliked Gingrich. Representative Carrie Meek, a Florida Democrat, charged Gingrich of signing a book deal that would bring him "a whole lot of [gold] dust." Her words were taken down. In another case, Democrats brought to the House floor a blown-up front page from the *New York Daily News* showing Gingrich in diapers and carrying the headline "Cry Baby." The chair had to banish the blowup from the floor. In this series of episodes, Martin Hoke, a former Republican congressman from Ohio, was reprimanded three times for accusing the Democrats of "lies" and "great hypocrisy." And

Congressman James Moran, Democrat from Virginia, and Randy "Duke" Cunningham, the former Republican congressman from California convicted for bribery, questioned each other's patriotism on American military involvement, "prompting Moran to shove Cunningham in the back on the way out of the chamber, triggering an indecorous melee involving a half-dozen members."[17]

There were other instances as well. In another episode in 1995, a tussle occurred between Dick Armey, the former Republican majority leader from Texas, and Frank, an openly gay member of the House. The two men rarely got along with each other. In one quarrel, Armey called Frank "Barney Fag." In another incident, also aimed at Frank, during a 1998 speech to cancer patients at the San Diego Rehabilitation Institute, the aforementioned Cunningham made a crude remark about Frank's sexuality, saying a rectal procedure he had received for his prostate surgery was "just not natural, unless maybe you're Barney Frank." At the same event, during the question-and-answer period, Cunningham was criticized by a questioner about his opposition to military spending cuts. In response to that, the former congressman "made a hand gesture and swore at the man." After the event, Cunningham apologized, saying, "I am sorry. I was out of line. I just get upset when people start bashing our military."[18]

Another Republican senator famous for his acerbic tone was Alfonse D'Amato, the former senator from New York. In his memoirs published in 1995, he described his former Senate colleagues in less than charitable ways, calling Ted Kennedy, the senior Democrat from Massachusetts, "an extreme, disingenuous partisan," Howard Metzenbaum, the former Democrat from Ohio, "a dictator," and the members of Congress collectively as a "bunch of turkeys."[19] Needless to say, such remarks never endeared D'Amato to his colleagues.

In another example, Representative James Leach, a respected centrist Republican from Iowa, relays an episode of unruly behavior on the House floor in the early 1990s. One day, then Congressman Dornan, a known conservative, rose not only to debate with fellow Congressman Steve Gunderson, Republican from Wisconsin, but also "to deride him as gay."[20] In response, the presiding officer dismissed Dornan from the House floor "for an act of unprecedented incivility—the outing of a colleague."[21] That same week, to quell the issue, Gunderson went public about his personal lifestyle, but according to Leach, "the notion that a Member could not respect a fellow Member's lifestyle remains one of the most chilling reminders that civility has more to do with gentility than partisanship."[22]

The new millennium ushered in increased instances of incivility in both houses of Congress. In an election year, in 2000, the rancor between the two parties' leaders inched up to higher decibel levels. On the House side, the relationship between then Democratic leader Richard Gephardt of Missouri and former GOP leader Newt Gingrich had been cold and stormy. Gingrich's successor as speaker of the House, J. Dennis Hastert, however, enjoys the reputation of a calmer individual, willing to negotiate and less prone to hostile and terse rhetoric.

But soon after taking over the speaker's job, even Hastert and Gephardt began to trade barbs. Writing in 2000 for the *Washington Post,* Eric Planin and Juliet Eilperin observed that the relationship between the two leaders had "gone from bad to worse....The two have not spoken directly on most of the major issues awaiting congressional action....Aides to the two leaders do little to disguise their bosses' contempt for each other. And recently, Gephardt has peppered Hastert with letters criticizing his leadership." According to John Feehery, spokesman for the speaker, "It's pretty clear Mr. Gephardt wants to stop everything we're doing. Every time the speaker has tried to reach out to him, he's got his hand slapped." In response, Gephardt is quoted to have said, "Frankly, the relationship is really no different than it was with Newt Gingrich. Their definition of bipartisanship is, 'My way or the highway.'"[23]

The relationship between these two leaders continued to be sour, for which Hastert appears not to be remorseful. In a September 22, 2000, interview with Karen Foerstel of the *Congressional Quarterly Weekly Report,* Hastert is quoted to have said: "I think trust is a two-way street. It kind of limits your ability to negotiate and work with somebody whose sole purpose is to try to make this House fail." According to Foerstel, "[t]he poor relationship between Hastert and Gephardt has not helped the parties cooperate. The two rarely meet and have dislike for each other that extends beyond politics. 'There's not much of a relationship,' Hastert said of Gephardt. The Speaker blamed the ill will on Gephardt, charging the Democrat with blocking legislation in order to label Republicans as a 'do-nothing Congress.'"[24]

During the 2000 election season, the speaker of the House took an extremely unusual step, something never done before. He openly campaigned against Gephardt. Hastert traveled to Gephardt's district in Missouri and publicly supported his challenger, something considered to be totally out of character for the leader of one party to do to that of another and represented a significant departure from the accepted rules of behavior. The speaker's move was taken by Gephardt as "a personal affront," and according to Foerstel, represented "a broader indication of the bitter legislative atmosphere."[25] Such conduct, nevertheless, would continue (as described later in this chapter when former Senate Majority Leader Bill Frist campaigned against former Senate Minority Leader Tom Daschle in South Dakota in 2004), further alienating the two parties and poisoning the relationship between the two leaders.

On the Senate side, the decibel levels were even higher in the new millennium, as if to one-up the House of Representatives. On May 17, 2000, then the two leaders of the Senate, Republican Trent Lott and Democrat Tom Daschle, locked into a quarrel over the refusal of the GOP majority to allow the Democratic minority to offer amendments to unrelated bills. Eric Schmitt, writing for the *New York Times*, captured the scene in detail. This is a good example of the increasingly vocal exchange between the two parties' leaders. According to Schmitt, the dialogue between Lott and Daschle became "unusually acrid... with rhetorical eye-gouging" as they "lobbed verbal volleys at each other in an angry, arm-waving screaming match...that launched a thousand insults."[26]

Schmitt relays this dialogue as follows, also found in the *Congressional Record*. After arguing over proposals on gun safety legislation, Lott said, "There were a number of things said earlier today on which I just bit my lip and took it because I thought, for the greater good of the Chamber, we should get an agreement and more forward....I also feel personally maligned, and I do not appreciate it."

An angry Senator Lott continues:

> I do not think we have any...God-given rights in this institution. We all have certain rights, and I am going to work to protect those rights....I am getting really tired of people questioning my commitment to the Senate and to the opportunity for debates....I tell you, what I am trying to do is find a way for the Senate to do its work. These charges that are leveled against me are nonsense....People talk about that civility has broken down, and there is acrimony. That is ridiculous. I think we have a very good relationship here....What it is really all about is getting the work of the Senate done, dealing with real bills and real issues, not playing games....As far as order and comity, I support that. I am going to do everything I can to continue to support that. But I think for us to have basically 1, 2, 3, 4 days tied up having debate on gun amendments instead of having debate on Kosovo and the military construction appropriations bill is not the way we should be operating.

Lott, sounding hurt, adds: "I have to go on the record saying I do believe I have been maligned unfairly. I have bent over backward to try to give notice when we were going to call up a bill and to have cooperation with the Democratic leadership to make sure Senators had a chance to make their case."

Finally, sarcastically, Lott ends his round: "But to come in here and think we have to have a right to offer non-germane amendments to every appropriations bill that comes through, and then criticize us for not getting our work done—oh, boy, that is really smart—really smart. Yes, we demand our rights to offer our issues. By the way, why aren't you guys getting those bills done? I do not believe the American people are being fooled by all of this."

Then it was Daschle's turn. He began,

> Let me just say the majority leader was able to get some things off his chest....I will tell you this. The way the Senate is being run is wrong. No majority leader in history has attempted to constrain Senate debate as aggressively as Senator Lott has chosen to do....That is his right. He has chosen the way he runs the Senate. I think he is doing that for what many believe is a laudatory reason. He is trying to protect his members so they don't have to vote on tough issues....But no majority leader has ever gone to the extent that he has.

Getting more angry and emotional for emphasis, Daschle continues:

> Why do we want to have debate on amendments? Because that is the only ability for the minority to express itself. The majority leader has phrased it very interestingly. He said: I don't want all these amendments to cause trouble. The more they cause trouble, the more in jeopardy the bills will be.... Over and over and over and over again, we are told that is the way it is going to be. One of our colleagues the other day said it is like the frog sitting in a pot of water who doesn't notice that the water keeps getting hotter and ultimately the frog boils to death. Well, the water continues to heat, and we are slowly boiling to death, procedurally....I hope, when we are in the majority, we understand the rights of the minority. I will admonish my colleagues to do that. But this is getting to be more and more a second House of Representatives. This is getting to be more and more a gagged body.

Daschle ends his round with a threatening tone: "[w]e have drawn the line. We are not going to be conducting business as we have in the last several months. That is over. That is behind us. We can do it the Senate way, or we are not going to do it at all."

Lott takes his turn and lobes the grenade back:

> If that is the way it is going to be, then that is the way it is going to be....I am
> not going to be threatened and intimidated by the minority in trying to get
> our work done. If you want to go through this approach, if you want to shut
> down everything, then everybody loses in the process. We can cooperate
> and we can get these bills done....But on both sides, we have Senators
> who want to offer things that will cause mischief and delay or kill a bill....
> I have tried to avoid having an acrimonious relationship. Maybe it is
> unavoidable in this election year, but I think that would be a shame for
> the American people because, after all, that is about whom we should be
> thinking....But if we are going to hold our breath, turn red in the face and
> threaten, then that is the way it will be. But everybody needs to understand
> that in that kind of relationship nobody wins; everybody loses.

Daschle, having calmed down a bit, returns his verbal assault in kind: "Let me just say no one wants to stomp their feet and get red in the face—certainly not me. That is not my style. If it has happened, it is only because the frustration level continues to mount....I am not trying to get excited here. But let me just say as softly and as sincerely as I can: That is not cooperation. That is a Senate version of dictatorship that I think is unacceptable."[27]

The two men butted heads again just a few weeks later. In early June 2000, Lott again expressed his frustration at the Democrats. "The last couple of weeks before we went out have been the most obstructionist I've ever seen them. I don't think it's in anybody's best interest for the Senate to be balled up with obstructionism on either side." Daschle lamented, "This has been probably the most damaging to the Senate institutionally that I can recall," referring to Lott's approach to running the Senate.[28]

A number of unsavory episodes on the Hill have involved Bill Thomas, a former GOP congressman from California, one-time chair of the coveted House Ways and Means Committee, who was pupiled in the Gingrich school of politics. In one case in 1995, Thomas, when he was chairman of the Ways and Means Subcommittee on Health, was seen by the House Democrats as being secretive about the Republican plan for reforming Medicare, holding just a single day of hearing, and generally dragging his feet on health care legislation. One day, Representative Sam Gibbons, the ordinarily genial Democrat from Florida and himself former chairman of the House Ways and Means Committee when the Democrats were in charge, upset by the stalling tactics, called Thomas and his Republican colleagues "a bunch of fascists."[29]

In what followed, Gibbons grabbed Thomas by his tie. After calming down, "Gibbons offered to buy Thomas a new tie...but otherwise appeared unrepentant." He continued,

> Does anybody know when we're going to have a bill and a hearing together? Last year [referring to when Gibbons was shepherding President Clinton's health care plan as chairman of the House Ways and Means Committee] I laboriously laid out what I had in mind. I listened to opposition from the Republicans in that committee room for hours on end, never cut one of them off. I have to think that their whole program of not having a piece of legislation, of always having spin doctors out there, of stalling and stalling and stalling, is not an accident, but a very deliberative plot to put their program over before the American people have any chance of understanding how it affects them.[30]

In a childish bit of revenge-seeking mood, Thomas sought to turn off House microphones one Saturday to prevent Democrats from speaking, and then ordered the House restaurants to close and deny service to the Democrats.[31] For their part, the Democrats held their own hearings outside "because the Republican leadership would not give the Democrats any space in the Capitol,"[32] another bit of childish play.

In another episode involving Thomas, his uncivil ways continued. In another quarrel with Democrats many years later when he was chair of the House Ways and Means Committee, Thomas called the Capitol Police to extricate Democratic members of his panel from the Ways and Means library during a markup on July 18, 2003. The Democrats used this instance to accuse the GOP of using heavy-handed tactics to govern the House. Indeed, the Republicans themselves were recipients of such dictatorial tactics when Democrats were in charge of the House. In this case, the GOP leaders, fearing reprisals in public response, pressured Thomas to apologize. Chairman Thomas made a public statement from the House floor on July 23, 2003, in which he said: "Because of my poor judgment, those outside the House who want to trivialize, marginalize and debase this institution were given an opportunity to do so....[W]hen you're charged and entrusted with responsibilities by you, my colleagues, as I have been, you deserve better. Moderation is required."[33]

In this vitriolic environment, members are quick to blame the other side for failures, without seeing their own faults. Senator Mitch

McConnell, Republican from Kentucky, took the Senate floor on November 10, 2003, to respond to Democratic complaints about the Senate Republican leadership. In his remarks, the senator compared GOP leader Frist's stewardship of the Senate with that of Senator Daschle, then the Democratic leader of the Senate:

> Well, Mr. President...let us recall that this leader [Senator Frist] is laboring under a one-vote margin, just as the last leader had to endure. Given that same burden, it might be appropriate and timely to compare the hard facts. Those hard facts deal with the passage of bills through the Senate. With the same one-vote majority, Senator Frist has pushed 10 appropriations bills across the Senate floor while last year's leadership delivered only 3. That is over three times as many appropriations bills through the Senate in this year compared to last year....Again, last year, three appropriations bills moved through the Senate, the worst record in at least two decades. Let me repeat that, Mr. President. Last year only three appropriations bills made it through the Senate, the worst record in at least two decades.... What is amateur, to use the Democratic leadership's terminology, is not doing your job and blaming someone else. That is what is amateur, not doing your job and blaming someone else.[34]

This statement reflects a frequent criticism of the modern-day Congress that each person or party work long and hard to protect their positions, often by finding faults in others.

Revenge, or promises of it, is yet another quality often displayed by the new crowd. Toward the end of the marathon filibuster launched by the Republicans in the Senate concerning judicial nominations in November 2003, Rick Santorum, former Republican senator from Pennsylvania, then one of the leaders of the filibuster, claimed on the Senate floor:

> What we are doing here is playing with real bullets. I tell you there are folks on our side of the aisle who are loving what you are doing. They are loving what you are doing, man. They just think, go, baby, go. Do this because we can't wait to get our arms around the next Democratic president who wants to stack the court with a bunch of people who believe God does not belong in the Pledge of Allegiance....We can't wait to get our arms around people who find in this Constitution things that are not in it, who believe it is their job to be the super senator, the super legislator, the super president. We can't wait to block those nominees because, do you know what, you did it first. You did it first. You can say, oh, no, we didn't do it first. You did it first.

You crossed the line. Oh, it has been threatened. It has been talked about around here. I will not deny that. I talked about it.[35]

Another GOP senator, Lindsey Graham of South Carolina, was no less cavalier on the Senate floor in the early morning hours of November 13, 2003: "If you don't think down the road it will be answered in kind by the Republican Party, I think you are very naïve. The animosity being generated by this practice [filibustering judicial nominees] is red hot among both bases, and it will be almost impossible, in my opinion, for this not to become the norm. Payback is hell."[36]

In a further escalation of the partisanship on the Hill, in 2004 then Senate Majority Leader Frist became the first Senate leader to campaign against his counterpart. Frist traveled to South Dakota and actively stumped for John Thune in a bid to unseat Daschle. This had never happened before, but is likely to happen again, representing yet another behavior that would put even more distance between the two parties. In his farewell address to the Senate, Daschle sadly said:

> Several months ago, I came to the floor and gave a speech at this desk expressing the hope that regardless of how the election turned out, we could continue mightily to search for the politics of common ground....If I could leave this body with one wish, it would be that we never give up that search for common ground....The politics of common ground will not be found on the far right or on the far left. That is not where most Americans live. We will only find it in the firm middle ground of common sense and shared values.[37]

The invective, however, continues. In an episode, which occurred in 2004, Dick Cheney, the vice president of the United States, happened to be on the Senate floor and ran into Patrick Leahy, the Democratic senator from Vermont and then the ranking Democrat on the Senate Judiciary Committee. The animosity between the two men was relatively well-known, and in this instance it spilled over into a public clash. Earlier in the week, Leahy had criticized Cheney, Halliburton Co., the vice president's former employer, and accused Cheney of cronyism relative to the firm. In the encounter on the Senate floor, the vice president let loose, and said to Leahy, "Fuck yourself." Cheney was unapologetic in explaining his remark to the media later on, and said instead, "I expressed myself rather forcefully, felt better after I had done it." He continued, "Ordinarily I don't express myself in strong terms, but I thought it was appropriate here." In return, David Carle, spokesperson for Senator Leahy, added, "It appears the vice president's previous calls for civility are now inoperative."[38]

While Cheney may have felt better after he had done it, his use of the four-letter word was widely viewed as an issue of vulgarity and profanity. The vice president admitted as much himself. In their coverage of the story, Dana Milbank and Helen Dewar, two *Washington Post* writers, began their report as follows: "Vice President Cheney on Friday vigorously defended his vulgarity directed at a prominent Democratic senator earlier this week in the Senate chamber. Cheney said he 'probably' used an obscenity in an argument Tuesday on the Senate floor...and added that he had no regrets."[39] According to presidential scholar James Pfiffner, this insult was "particularly egregious because it was not a comment about a third party but stated directly to the person insulted; it was not private, but public; it was said on the floor of Congress; and it was said publicly by the president of the Senate, the vice president of the United States."[40]

Cheney, however, is known for having a sharp tongue. In the 1980s, as a member of the Republican minority in the House, Cheney would occasionally lob grenades at the Democratic leaders. In one incident, complaining about the autocratic rule by the House Democrats, Cheney, then a Republican congressman from Wyoming and the House minority whip, in a quarrel over a procedural issue concerning a tax bill, called Wright, then the House speaker, "a heavy-handed son of a bitch [who] will do anything he can to win at any price."[41]

In recent times, the vice president has gotten into verbal fights with Charles Rangel, a Democratic congressman from New York. In a bit of a smear campaign as a prelude to the 2006 midterm elections, Cheney said that the liberal Harlem lawmaker, as the incoming chair of the vaunted House Ways and Means Committee, would increase taxes and ruin the economy if the Democrats win back the House, with the vice president's remarks "intended to raise fears about Rangel, as well as other prominent Democrats, as a way to convince voters to stop them from taking over the House." Rangel shot back: "He's such a real son of a bitch, he just enjoys a confrontation." Rangel further noted that Cheney "may need to go to 'rehab' for 'whatever personality deficit he may have suffered.'" Asked whether he was again implying that Cheney was "mentally ill," Rangel quipped, "I don't think he's shot anyone in the face lately [referring to the vice president's accidental shooting of his friend, Harry Whittington, earlier in 2006], so I'll give him the benefit of the doubt."[42]

In 2005, Rangel had launched other verbal grenades at Cheney. He remarked that the vice president, who has suffered four heart attacks, "was too sick to work." Rangel said, "I would like to believe he's sick rather than just mean and evil. Sometimes I don't even think Cheney is awake enough to know what's going on." Cheney responded, "I'm frankly surprised at his comments....They were so out of line it almost struck me that...Charlie was having some problem. Charlie is losing it, I guess."[43]

In another unsavory incident, Democratic Senate leader Harry Reid, in a classroom talk on civics with a group of high school students in his home state of Nevada, called President Bush "a loser." "The man's father is a wonderful human being," stated Senator Reid. "I think this guy is a loser."[44] After realizing what he had done, the senator called Bush to apologize about his remark. However, when asked about his comment a few days later, the senator responded: "I tell people how I feel about things. I don't try to hide how I feel. Maybe my choice of words was improper, and I have indicated that maybe they were, but I want everyone here, I repeat, to know I'm going to continue to call things the way that I see them, and I think this administration has done a very, very bad job for this nation and the world."[45]

In another episode involving Reid, he charged the Bush administration as one of the dirtiest in memory, and the Republicans as among the most corrupt. According to Reid, "[t]he idea of Republicans reforming themselves is like asking John Gotti to clean up organized crime. I thought I'd seen the last of corruption when I helped clean up Las Vegas thirty years ago. But, while its not quite the mafia of Las Vegas in the 1970s, what is happening today in Washington is every bit as corrupt and the consequences for our country have been just as severe."[46]

A week later, in a speech to the liberal Center for American Progress, Senator Reid lambasted the Bush administration once again. In this speech, the Democratic leader provided a comprehensive indictment of the administration. Resounding the theme of corruption, he said:

> Republicans today control the House of Representatives, the Senate and the White House. They have absolute power, and it has corrupted their Party and led to the culture of corruption that we see now in Washington. We have the Republican leader of the House of Representatives [referring to Tom DeLay], admonished three times for ethics violation and under indictment now for money laundering. We have the White House, where an employee has been indicted for the first time in 135 years [referring to

Lewis Libby, Vice President Dick Cheney's former chief-of-staff]. There's Karl Rove, who is under investigation...and David Safavian, the man appointed by President Bush to be in charge of hundreds of billions of dollars in government contracts who was led away in handcuffs because of his dealings with Jack Abramoff and others. And then, we have the Republican "K-Street Project," which has invited lobbyists inside our nation's Capitol...as long as they are willing to pay the right price. The Republican abuse of power comes at great cost to our country, and we can see it in the present state of our union. Special interests and the well-connected have grown stronger, while our national security...our economy...our health care...and our government have grown weaker.... Republicans run good campaigns, but when it comes to actually governing and protecting Americans, they have a record of incompetence.[47]

The vituperation continues!

In early 2007, the Hill Democrats engaged in one of their usual war of words with the administration over its Iraq policy. The Democrats wanted to impose troop withdrawal deadlines on an Iraq funding bill, which the administration vehemently opposed. The president and the vice president vigorously defended their approach of not having any deadlines and chided the Democrats on this issue. To which Senator Reid responded, "The president sends out his attack dog often. That's also known as Dick Cheney." The senator further added, "I'm not going to get into a name-calling match with somebody who has a 9 percent approval rating."[48]

In yet another episode, in early 2006, Democratic Senator Hillary Clinton, the junior senator from New York, lashed out at the Republican-controlled House of Representatives and the Bush administration. In a speech honoring Martin Luther King Jr., Clinton said: "When you look at the way the House of Representatives has been run, it has been run like a plantation, and you know what I'm talking about. It has been run in a way so that nobody with a contrary view has had a chance to present legislation, to make an argument, to be heard." Regarding the Bush administration, she offered the following: "We have a culture of corruption, we have cronyism, we have incompetence. I predict to you that this administration will go down in history as one of the worst that has ever governed our country."[49]

These comments drew sharp retort from the Republicans in the House, who accused Senator Clinton of playing the race card. Speaker Hastert replied: "I've never run a plantation before. I'm not even sure of what kind of association she's trying to make. If she's trying to be racist, I think that's unfortunate, but I'm not going to comment any further on that." Peter King, a Republican House member from New York, added: "It's definitely using the race card. It definitely has racist connotations. She knows it. She knew the audience. She knew what she was trying to say, and it was wrong. And she should be ashamed."[50]

Meanwhile, in another incident on the Hill, Senator Russ Feingold, a Democrat from Wisconsin and a member of the Senate Judiciary Committee, publicly clashed with Senator Arlen Specter, a Republican from Pennsylvania and then the chairman of the Senate Judiciary Committee. The incident involved a constitutional amendment to ban same-sex marriage, which Senator Specter had called up and the committee approved by a party-line vote of 10-8. The senator from Wisconsin, who was then thinking of running for the presidency in 2008, feeling very strongly about this issue, angrily "declared his opposition to the amendment, his affinity for the Constitution and his intention to leave the meeting." Specter shouted back, "I don't need to be lectured by you. You are no more a protector of the Constitution than am I. If you want to leave, good riddance." Before storming out, Feingold retorted, "I've enjoyed your lecture, too, Mr. Chairman."[51]

Last but not least, after the 2006 midterm congressional elections, Senator James Webb, the newly elected senator from Virginia, went to the White House to attend a reception hosted by President Bush for the newest members of Congress. At this event, Webb "declined to stand in a presidential receiving line or to have his picture taken with the man he had often criticized on the stump" during the election. Bush, however, soon found him and he asked, "How's your boy?" referring to the senator's son, serving as a Marine in Iraq. Webb replied, "I'd like to get them out of Iraq, Mr. President." The president then said, "That's not what I asked you. How's your boy?" To which, Webb coldly responded, "That's between me and my boy, Mr. President," ending the conversation.[52]

—◆—

On December 20, 1995, Senator Robert Byrd, the veteran Democrat from West Virginia and a former leader of his party, took the Senate floor to speak about "Civility in the Senate":

> Mr. President, I rise today to express my deep concern at the growing incivility in this chamber....Mr. President, can't we rein in our tongues and lower our voices and speak to each other and about each other in a more civil fashion?...Have civility and common courtesy and reasonableness

taken leave of this chamber? Surely the individual vocabularies of members of this body have not deteriorated to the point that we can only express ourselves in such crude and coarse and offensive language....Can we no longer engage in reasoned, even intense, partisan exchanges in the Senate without imputing evil motives to other senators, without castigating the personal integrity of our colleagues? Such utterly reckless statements can only poison the waters of the well of mutual respect and comity which must prevail in this body if our two political parties are to work together in the best interests of the people whom we serve....Mr. President, it is with profound sadness that I have taken the floor today to express my alarm and concern at the poison that has settled in this chamber. There have been giants in this Senate, and I have seen some of them. Little did I know when I came here that I would live to see pygmies stride like colossuses while marveling, like Aesop's fly, sitting on the axle of a chariot, "My, what a dust I do raise!"....I understand, and we understand, that partisanship plays a part in our work here....There is nothing inherently wrong with partisanship. But I hope that we will all take a look at ourselves on both sides of this aisle and understand also that we must work together in harmony and with mutual respect for one another. This very charter of government under which we live was created in a spirit of compromise and mutual concession. And it is only in that spirit that a continuance of this charter of government can be prolonged and sustained....Let us stop this seemingly irresistible urge to destroy all that we have always held sacred. Let us cease this childish need to resort to emotional strip-tease on the Senate floor.[53]

Others have echoed Senator Byrd's reflections.

Upon his return to the Senate in 1998, former Senate majority leader Mike Mansfield, Democrat from Montana, admonished senators about bickering and partisanship. He is reported to have told the senators that they

must embrace their collective duty to work on behalf of the nation, which he said "can prevail only if there is a high degree of accommodation, mutual restraint, and a measure of courage...in all of us. It can prevail only if we recognize that, in the end, it is not the senators as individuals who are of fundamental importance. In the end, it is the institution of the Senate. It is the Senate itself as one of the foundations of the Constitution. It is the Senate as one of the rocks of the Republic."[54]

Mansfield further noted "the importance of respecting the institution and the people who serve there."[55]

CHAPTER 3

CHANGING OF THE GUARD

The world is grown so bad,
That wrens make prey where eagles dare not perch:
Since every Jack became a gentleman,
There's many a gentle person made a Jack.

> William Shakespeare, *King Richard III*, act 1,
> sc. 3, 70–73

Politics and governing demand compromise. But these
Christians believe they are acting in the name of God, so they
can't and won't compromise. I know, I've tried to deal with
them.

> Barry Goldwater, former Republican
> senator from Arizona

In his book entitled *Faith and Politics*, John Danforth, former Republican senator from Missouri, observes:

> When I arrived in Washington in January 1977, I was in the philosophical center of a broad range of Republican senators. To my left were people many Republicans today would call liberals: Jacob Javits of New York, Clifford Case of New Jersey, Edward Brooke of Massachusetts and Lowell Weicker of Connecticut. To my right were conservative stalwarts, including Barry Goldwater of Arizona, Strom Thurmond of South Carolina, Jesse Helms of North Carolina and John Tower of Texas. Then there were the senators who, with me, were somewhere in the center of our party, people like Howard Baker of Tennessee, Bob Dole and his Kansas colleague Jim Pearson. Of course, such diverse Republicans had differences of opinion on various issues, but we respected each other and we respected our differences....Since that time, the breadth of the Republican Party has narrowed. Gone are Javits, Case and Brooke; gone are Baker, Dole and Danforth. The band of Republican senators most people would call moderate now numbers a half dozen or so, and many would say good riddance.[1]

It is a well-known fact that the Congress of the United States has altered remarkably during the postwar years. All things change, and Congress has been no exception. The question is, has Congress transformed for the better or for the worse?

Some truisms about the old Congress. The Congress of the 1950s, 1960s, and 1970s was guided by principles of camaraderie, politeness, courteousness, and civility. Members generally respected each other, got along with each other, and socialized with each other. Despite their political differences, members cooperated with each other. It was understood that one may not need his or her political opponent today on a bill but may need the same person tomorrow on another bill. Need and/or want brought members together.

Some truisms about the new Congress. The world of Congress in the 1980s and 1990s was guided by principles of name-calling, finger-pointing, revenge, and the vernacular of street fighting. Members in this era could care less about cultivating relationships with the other side. Most members choose not to believe in bipartisanship and compromise. Most have significantly lowered the level of debate. Neither need nor want unites members in this era.

Chapter 2 highlighted the growing uncivil debate. My goal in this chapter is to identify the changing personalities in Congress over the past fifty years and how they either refrained from, or contributed to, increases in uncivil debate. This chapter distinguishes the "old style" member of Congress from the "new style" member. Based upon my observations, I have created lists of prominent members known for their bipartisanship and civility in the old days and for their lack of it in these days.[2] The focus in this chapter is on this list of selected individuals that exemplify the two styles of behavior. I shall draw the implications of this changing behavior in the concluding section of this chapter.

———————

The following qualities characterized the members of the old guard: friendship, respect, and comity. These were the prized commodities in those days.

In the old days, remarked an observer of Congress, freshmen members of the House were lectured about the importance of having collegial relationships:

> Making friends with his colleagues is a most important activity indeed, and he should develop friendly relationships with committee and

House staff and agency personal as well. The resourceful beginner will learn that the cornerstones of success are, in fact, hard work and making friends....Because so much of a legislator's time is spent in close association with colleagues, and because their cooperation is so often required if he is to succeed, freshman members are especially cautioned about intragroup relationships.[3]

The importance of friendship, in other words, was considered vital to a successful legislative life. Donald Matthews' observations about amiable legislative atmosphere in the Senate of the 1950s are well-known to students of Congress.[4]

A notable feature of the old guard was that they kept things positive about Congress and legislative work. Rarely did members choose to deride the opposition for legislative failures. Such statements were positive even by members of the minority party, which would be an utter surprise today. Consider, for example, the statement put out by the House Republican Policy Committee on December 4, 1967, commenting on the 1967 legislative work in the House. The statement read that the House GOP, a minority then, had "compiled a remarkable record of achievement and progress." Congressman John Rhodes, Republican of Arizona and then chairman of the Policy Committee, noted that his committee had "'adopted 30 policy statement,' of which 24 became the subject of House roll-call votes. The Republican position was upheld on 18 of the 24 votes." On the same day, then House Minority Leader Gerald Ford, Republican of Michigan, told reporters that "I think it has been a good Congress."[5]

Others frequently made similar positive statements in those days about Congress and its work. Reacting to the same 1967 session, Senate Majority Leader Mike Mansfield, Democrat of Montana, noted: "It has been a respectable, decent Congress. No real high points. This year gave us a chance to sit back, ruminate and cogitate a bit." Then Senate Minority Leader Everett McKinley Dirksen, Republican of Illinois, commented that the Congress had been "impressive because of what it has deliberately resisted in the way of legislation." Congressmen Carl Albert, Democrat of Oklahoma and then House majority leader, echoed similar congratulatory sentiments.[6]

Indeed, the contrast between then and now is vividly summarized by former Indiana Democrat Lee Hamilton, an insider and once a respected member of the House who belonged to the old guard. In his commentaries on Congress published in 2004, Hamilton wrote:

Not long ago I was asked to give a talk on how Congress has changed since 1965, the year I entered it as a young freshman member from southern Indiana. As I sat looking through my old speeches, a phrase jumped out at me. Congress, I told my audiences back then, did its work in an "extraordinarily hospitable atmosphere." Indeed, I liked to say, no matter how spirited the policy debate, "a cocoon of warmth" surrounded us....If I suggested anything of the sort today I'd be laughed out of the room. The last several years have been particularly divisive and partisan. Certainly tough times in Congress are nothing new....Yet, during my time in Congress, I witnessed a marked change in its atmosphere: the demonization of people in the other party, nasty personal attacks, a willingness to pull out all the stops to undermine the other side's agenda, and concerted efforts to topple the other party's leader....Breakdowns in civility are among the most serious threats to the ability of Congress to work well. Spirited, even heated debates and aggressively pushing the interests of your constituents are to be expected and are healthy to the institution. That's how issues get thrashed out in a democratic society. But personal attacks and excessive partisanship poison the atmosphere of Congress and undermine the ability of members to come together to do the nation's business....Back in the days of that "warm cocoon," when I was still learning my way around Congress, I made a mistake on the House floor. I was managing a bill for the Democrats, and I forgot a small parliamentary move that would have locked victory in place. William Bray, a prominent Republican who was also from Indiana, came over to me, put his arm on my shoulder, gently pointed out my blunder, and showed me how to fix it. And this was on a bill he *opposed*. That was how Congress worked then. (emphasis in original)[7]

This statement represents the old ways and the old guard, where members were willing to extend a helping hand to those across the aisle, where congeniality and bargaining prevailed, and where name-calling and accusations took the back seat.

Selected members of the old school highlighted in this chapter are listed in Table 3.1. They are widely known among political scientists, journalists, and in popular circles for their conciliatory tones. They valiantly epitomized the old era. These would be the Hall of Famers of that era. The listing has no particular order.

The important point that I wish to stress in this chapter is that what distinguishes these members from the new ones is not so much their partisanship, for they were sometimes very partisan also, but rather their openness to concede to camaraderie and civility at the end of the day. The old guard members did not see the world in black and

Table 3.1
Party Unity Scores for Leading Old Guard Members, 1950–2000

	Career Low	Career High	Career Average	Party Average
"Old School" Congressmen				
Carl Albert (D-OK)	47	100	85	78
Bill Archer (R-TX)	75	97	89	81
Tom Foley (D-WA)	58	100	82	78
Lee Hamilton (D-IN)	56	88	76	80
Joseph Martin (R-MA)	13	91	54	80
Bob Michel (R-IL)	54	89	77	78
Tip O'Neill (D-MA)	68	96	81	77
Sam Rayburn (D-TX)	79	88	84	77
John Rhodes (R-AZ)	44	97	70	78
Dan Rostenkowski (D-IL)	57	90	78	79
"Old School" Senators				
Howard Baker (R-TN)	43	90	70	79
John Breaux (D-LA)	59	84	71	85
John Chafee (R-RI)	29	75	55	81
Bill Cohen (R-ME)	39	69	58	81
Jack Danforth (R-MO)	41	85	71	79
Everett Dirksen (R-IL)	56	100	80	74
Lyndon Johnson (D-TX)	61	95	78	79
Mike Mansfield (D-MT)	61	100	79	76
Pat Moynihan (D-NY)	68	95	84	81
Warren Rudman (R-NH)	58	89	76	80

Note: Data stop at 2000 for those members who were still serving in 2000.

white, but rather in many shades of gray. Ideology was not their ultimate driving force, although they also vehemently debated the issues. They understood that partisanship went only so far. Indeed, what greased the wheels and produced successful legislative feats was cooperation, bargaining, and respect.

As Table 3.1 shows, in the old House, congressmen often had higher support for their party throughout their careers than the average support for their party during their years of service.[8] Carl Albert, for example, supported his party 85 percent of the time during his career, when the average support for the Democratic Party in the House was 78 percent. Albert, known as the "Little Giant," was renowned for working well with the other side, staying tough but cutting deals when necessary. Bill Archer, former Republican from Texas, saw virtues on both sides of the aisle and was a consummate deal-maker.

Yet, he averaged his career at 89 percent, when the average support for the GOP in the House was at 81 percent.

Tom Foley, former Democratic speaker of the House from Washington, was often criticized by his party's colleagues for being too conciliatory with the Republicans. However, particularly as a leader, he understood the need for congeniality. At the same time, Foley favored his party's positions more than the average Democrat. He voted with his party 82 percent of the time, with the party average being at 78 percent. Tip O'Neill, also former Democratic speaker of the House from Massachusetts, was similarly cordial with the GOP. He was on extremely friendly terms with Republican Minority Leader Bob Michel, "who were golfing partners during the early 1980s."[9] But, O'Neill too stood at 81 percent support for the Democrats during his career, when his party stood at 77 percent.

It is said that Sam Rayburn, former Democratic speaker of the House from Texas, was married to the House. The popular saying "to get along, you have to go along" is often attributed to him. Rayburn epitomized reconciliation and compromise. However, he also voiced support for his party more than the other Democrats, backing his party 84 percent of the time throughout his career, while his Democratic colleagues voted for the party 77 percent of the time.

Others in the old guard happen to register less support for their party throughout their careers than the party average during their years in the House, yet are known as solid partisans and for getting along with the other side. Among them was Lee Hamilton, known throughout his career in Congress for interest and expertise in foreign affairs. He endorsed his party's positions 76 percent of the time during his tenure in the House, with the party average at 80 percent. He was also widely known and often spoke out about compromise and reaching out to the other side both during his career and after leaving Congress.[10] Indeed, his bipartisan demeanor led to his selection as cochair of the sensitive 9/11 Commission by Republican President George Bush. Also among them was Joseph Martin, former GOP congressman from Massachusetts. Martin, a Republican leader, often enjoyed friendly relations with Rayburn, a Democratic leader. Martin vastly undersupported his party in his career, standing at 54 percent, with the rest of his colleagues endorsing the Republican positions at an 80 percent clip.

Bob Michel, former Republican from Illinois and minority leader of his party in the House, was widely touted for this moderation. In 1994, what turned out to be a banner year for the GOP in the House, Michel chose not to seek reelection for his seat from Illinois, citing increased bitterness and personality conflicts on the Hill. Michel's support for his party was very similar to the GOP average during his career, standing at 77 versus 78 percent, respectively. Commentators spoke of Michel in glowing terms upon his retirement from the House. Sam Donaldson on *This Week with David Brinkley* said:

> Bob Michel is a great guy but his time was up. He was a moderate, and it's the unmoderates who control the House Republicans, that is, the Newt Gingriches of the world, the firebomb throwers: burn this village in order to save it, destroy the House in order to try to elect Republicans, have term limitations....Bomb throwers don't believe in civility, bomb throwers believe in throwing bombs...opposing every principle of the other party simply for partisan opposition.[11]

On the same ABC show, Cokie Roberts stated: "With the end of Bob Michel, what you really see is the end of civility in the House of Representatives in a very important way and that's what he represented and it's a sad day to see him go."[12]

John Rhodes of Arizona represented similar political philosophy. Much like many congressional leaders of that era, he often took heat from his GOP colleagues for not fighting with the Democrats. Indeed, one observer described Rhodes as "one in a chain of GOP leaders who sought bipartisan comity in the House despite recurring criticism of that strategy from agitators within the party, who saw the strategy as a route to perpetual standing as the minority party."[13] Rhodes supported his party positions less than the average Republicans, standing at his personal career average of 70 percent as opposed to 78 percent for the party average.

Last, in the House, Dan Rostenkowski, former Democrat from Illinois, also practiced politics in the bipartisan spirit for much of his career. Rostenkowski's support for his party was very close to the average for the rest of the House Democrats. He endorsed Democratic stands 78 percent of the time, with the party average at 79 percent. But, Rostenkowski, as chairman of the powerful House Ways and Means Committee, along with other influential Democratic committee chairs, is often cited for his lack of bipartisanship and comity in the 1980s and the early 1990s, contributing perhaps to the end of the Democratic reign in the House in 1994.

In the Senate, a vast majority of the old school senators were less supportive of their party than the party averages during their careers. The Senate has always been known for more bipartisanship than the

House. It is no surprise to begin this list with Howard Baker, former GOP leader from Tennessee. Known for his bipartisanship and widely respected across the aisle, Baker voted with his party 70 percent of the time, with the party average being 79 percent. John Breaux, a leading Democrat from Louisiana, stood with his party at 71 percent, with the rest of Senate Democrats endorsing the party positions at 85 percent. On the eve of his departure from the Hill in 2004, Breaux is quoted to have said: "I loved being in the middle. I loved to do the deal, and everybody knew it." In the same deal-making spirit, Breaux noted that his predecessor Senator Russell B. Long "could get more done in the afternoon, after work over a bottle of bourbon, talking with the other side. He could put a deal together, and I would argue the country wasn't any worse off for it."[14]

In the old days, the Southern Democrats often banded with the northern Republicans to create the political center. John Chafee, former Republican from Rhode Island, was known for building coalitions with the Democrats. Indeed, he stood with his party only 55 percent of the time, with his party average at 81 percent. Upon his retirement, E.J. Dionne of the *Washington Post* spoke in high praise for the departing senator's bipartisanship, whom he described as "a great problem-solver." Noted Dionne: "Progressive Republicans have been, on the whole, high-quality public servants with a capacity for civility, a tendency toward the practical, an interest in innovation and reform, and a gift for spotting flaws in the ideas of both parties. It makes you hope that John Chafee's Republican generation will not be the last of its kind."[15]

Another northeastern Republican, Bill Cohen from Maine, was viewed by many in equally praiseworthy terms throughout his Senate career. Cohen also voted much less with his party compared to his other GOP colleagues. During his tenure, he supported his party only 58 percent of the time, when his party stood at 81 percent. It was this ability to work with the other side that prompted former President Bill Clinton, a Democrat, to pick Cohen as his Secretary of Defense during his second term in office. Jack Danforth, a Missouri Republican, also garnered many brownie points for his ability to see all sides of the issues, for his thoughtfulness, and for his comity as a senator. He averaged his career support for the Senate Republicans at 71 percent, when his party was at 79 percent.

In a recent retrospective, Danforth, an Episcopal minister, derided members of his party for their conduct in recent years. He wrote in a *New York Times* editorial:

During the 18 years I served in the Senate, Republicans often disagreed with each other. But there was much that held us together. We believed in limited government, in keeping light the burden of taxation and regulation. We encouraged the private sector, so that a free economy might thrive. We believed that judges should interpret the law, not legislate. We were internationalists who supported an engaged foreign policy, a strong national defense and free trade. These were principles shared by virtually all Republicans. But in recent times, we Republicans have allowed this shared agenda to become secondary to the agenda of Christian conservatives. As a senator, I worried every day about the size of the federal deficit. I did not spend a single minute worrying about the effect of gays on the institution of marriage. Today it seems to be the other way around.[16]

As this statement indicates, partisanship and ideology are not what drove Danforth. Rather, he was motivated by a sense of objectivity and nonpartisanship.

In an interview, Danforth squarely blamed the newer member of his party, his "fellow Christians," for increased incivility and paralyzing polarization in Congress. He recalled "a more pleasant era of coalitions and compromises that gave way to ever fiercer partisanship starting in the early 1990s after Thomas [Supreme Court Justice Clarence Thomas] was already on the bench. He dates the beginning of the downslide to the arrival in the Senate of sharp-tongued former House Republicans." Indeed, Danforth has publicly argued that "the Republican right is a divisive force in the party and the nation. He [has] traced a relationship between increased activism by Christian conservatives and the collapse of collegiality."[17]

Another New Englander, Warren Rudman, former GOP senator from New Hampshire, was also less supportive of his party than the party average, endorsing the Republican positions 76 percent of the time, with the party average at 80 percent. Rudman expressed considerable disappointment in his party as well as his fellow partisans when he chose to resign in 1992 rather than seek a third term. Elected in 1980 to the Senate, Rudman always kept a sensible posture. He described his decision to depart Congress in the following terms:

The Republican Party I grew up with was starting to vanish: the party of Eisenhower, Taft, Dirksen and Baker, men who believed in a strong defense and less government, and who didn't think you could solve every problem by passing a law. If someone had told me in the 1960s that one day I would serve in a Republican Party that opposed abortion rights—which the

Supreme Court had endorsed—advocated prayer in the schools, and talked about government-inspired "family values," I would have thought he was crazy. . . . To me the essence of conservatism is just the opposite: Government should not intrude in anything as personal as the decision to have a child, it should not be championing prayer or religion, and family values should come from families and religious institutions, not from politically inspired, Washington-based moralists. . . . I thought the essence of good government was reconciling divergent views with compromises that served the country's interests. But that's not how movement conservatives or far-left liberals operate. The spirit of civility and compromise was drying up. By the 1990s, many nights I would go home and shake my head and think, We're not getting a hell of a lot done here. And then I would think, This isn't much fun.[18]

The "no fun" argument has been noted by others as well.

On the other hand, some senators in the old school were known not only for standing firmly with their party but also for cutting deals with the other side. Everett Dirksen supported his party a bit more than the party average (80 vs. 74 percent, respectively). Mike Mansfield supported the Democrats 79 percent of the time during his Senate career, with his party at 76 percent at that time. As a matter of fact, Mansfield was frequently lauded by his Democratic and Republican colleagues for his gentility, egalitarianism, and respect for the institution. He enjoyed a warm friendship with Dirksen, a fellow from across the aisle.

Daniel Patrick Moynihan, former Democrat from New York, usually practiced politics from both sides of the street. Observers noted that Moynihan "proudly displayed in his office framed covers of The Nation and The New Republic that branded him a 'neo-conservative' and a 'neo-liberal.' He was neo-neither."[19] In his Senate career, Moynihan supported Democratic positions on 84 percent of the votes, with his fellow colleagues standing at 81 percent. Upon his death in 2003, fellow Republican Senator Orrin Hatch of Utah, who knew him well, said that Moynihan "was willing to move to the center. He was one of the few who did when the chips were down."[20] Summarizing his decades of public service, conservative columnist George F. Will observed that Moynihan was "more conversant with, and more involved in, more of the nation's transforming controversies than anyone else. Who will do what he has done for the intellectual nutritiousness of public life? The nation is not apt to see his like again, never having seen it before him."[21]

Finally, perhaps the ultimate power broker of the old school, one who epitomized the art of politics, was none other than Lyndon Johnson, former Democratic Senate leader from Texas. Johnson was almost on par with his party, supporting the Democratic votes 78 percent of the time throughout his career, with the party average at 79 percent.

The party unity data noted above reveal that these respectable members often showed their willingness to deviate from their party and regularly worked to seek compromises with those across the aisle to get things done. Many were less supportive of their party than the party averages, some were more. However, they did not seem to care so about their party or their personal positions. Rather, they had the bigger picture in mind: the institution, the nation, and legislative success in the long run.

Indeed, in 1996, fourteen centrist senators of both parties left the Senate expressing similar frustrations, citing the lack of comity and paramount interests in personal concern rather than for the nation as the key reasons. In analyzing their farewell addresses, Norman Ornstein found a major theme, which was the focal reason for their departure: "it is a plea for the spirit of comity and compromise in our politics, and an underlying worry about the decline of civility, the collapse of the center, and the rise of partisanship and rigid ideology in our politics."[22]

———

On November 10, 2003, at the beginning of an unusual 40-hour marathon filibuster on judicial nominations, Dr. Barry C. Black, the chaplain of the Senate, offered a prayer that read in part:

> Long hours promise to test our patience and civility as unresolved issues seek to exasperate, producing discord. Help the Members of this body to sidestep the divisive power of contention and find common ground. Remind them that soft answers turn away anger. Destroy the winner-takes-all mentality and help them seek to understand before they are understood.... Make them exemplary models of reconciliation for a nation and world that watch their deliberations. May their serious efforts to build bridges have a ripple effect that will have a positive impact on our Nation and world.[23]

This admonition would serve well to all new-style members of Congress.

The "new school" of thought, nonetheless, is governed much by the principles that Thomas Hobbes described life would be in the state of nature: solitary, poor, nasty, brutish, and short. The new school's members practice in search and destroy tactics. The following traits define the members of the new guard: personal ambition, finger-pointing, and in-your-face attitude.[24]

Commenting on the new era of politicians, one reporter noted: "What is over is a generation and an attitude of members of Congress who had a love and a respect for the institution of Congress. In the freshmen, there's no institutional memory. In people such as Mr. Gingrich there is more desire just to confront for the sake of confrontation than there is to achieve something. And I think that's destructive of the House."[25] Gone are the days of institutional respect, collegial respect, and achieving progress for the nation.

Things have gotten really bad under the new guard. In 2000, a long-time political observer characterized the contemporary Senate in the following fashion:

> While they have not resorted to canes, pistols and fists as they did in the old days, senators are moving toward setting a new record for partisan combat, employing guerrilla tactics to surprise, intimidate and—if all else fails—exhaust their enemy. . . . The struggle plays out day after day in much the same way: Republicans bring up a bill. Democrats, waiting in the weeds, prepare to launch amendments on gun control or other issues that GOP senators do not want to vote on. Republicans make a preemptive strike by moving immediately to cut off all such amendments. Democrats cry foul, demand their rights and block further action. Republicans bring up another bill, and the whole process starts over again. . . . Through history, the Senate has often fallen short of its textbook image as a great debating society, where courtly members address one another as "my distinguished colleague" and discuss lofty issues in erudite terms.[26]

Similar sentiments were expressed elsewhere:

> Long viewed as the more dignified and cautious body of Congress, the Senate now finds itself mired in partisan, sand-lot warfare more typical of the House of Representatives. . . . The past few weeks in the Senate have been marked by an arm-waving screaming match between the Republican and Democratic leaders and a series of threats and counter-threats over spending bills that must be passed before the November election. The Senate has passed only a handful of significant bills this year, leaving things like increasing the minimum wage and cracking down on juvenile crime still in limbo. . . . The vitriol and partisanship between the two parties has reached new heights, casting a shadow on the Senate's reputation, or at least its self-image, for careful deliberation and effectiveness. . . . Republicans say

that the Democrats, rather than pushing for consensus, are behaving more like their rowdy counterparts in the House. All too often, Republicans argue, Democrats cavalierly slow things on the floor by attaching irrelevant amendments to important bills and by threatening filibusters so they can portray the Republicans as "do-nothing" senators in an election year.... "The last couple of weeks before we went out has been the most obstructionist I've ever seen them," said Senator Trent Lott of Mississippi, the majority leader, referring to Democratic senators. "I don't think it's in anybody's best interest for the Senate to be balled up with obstructionism on either side." For their part, Democrats say the Republicans have effectively gagged them and stifled thorough, deliberative discussion. They want Mr. Lott to loosen his hold and permit the Democrats to debate such issues as managed health care, gun control and the minimum wage. Until that happens, they say, they will continue to engage in parliamentary tactics.... Senator Tom Daschle of South Dakota, the Democratic leader, lamented Mr. Lott's style of running the Senate, arguing that denying the minority the chance to vote on its agenda has hurt the overall institution. "This has been probably the most damaging to the Senate institutionally that I can recall," Mr. Daschle said today, referring to Mr. Lott's method of limiting debate and refusing amendments. "If this practice continues, there really won't be any difference in how the Senate and House function."[27]

The scenario described here is repeated over and over again in today's Senate.

Table 3.2 highlights the selected members of the new school. They are widely known for their lack of bipartisanship and civility. They are commonly viewed as putting their personal and partisan interest above the national concerns. They are widely regarded as unyielding to the other side. They are the leading Hall of Famers of the new era.

Consider these numbers. In the House, until 2000, David Bonior, Democrat from Michigan, was considered to be one of the most partisan Democrats of the modern era. Bonior averaged 89 percent support for his party during his House career, with the party standing at 83 percent. On the GOP side, a congressman who could be described in similar terms is Dan Burton, Republican of Indiana. Burton is known to be ferociously partisan, who especially during the Clinton years became known for launching partisan attacks and investigations against the Clinton presidency. Referring to President Clinton, in April 1998 he told the *Indianapolis Star:* "This guy's a scumbag. That's why I'm after him."[28] His zealousness has not earned

Table 3.2
Party Unity Scores for Leading New Guard Members, 1950–2000

	Career Low	Career High	Career Average	Party Average
"New School" Congressmen				
David Bonior (D-MI)	79	97	89	83
Dan Burton (R-IN)	85	98	93	84
Tom DeLay (R-TX)	87	99	92	84
Bob Dornan (R-CA)	67	92	83	81
Newt Gingrich (R-GA)	71	97	84	81
Bob Livingston (R-LA)	41	92	77	82
David Obey (D-WI)	72	94	88	80
Nancy Pelosi (D-CA)	89	96	93	86
Bob Walker (R-PA)	84	98	93	81
Maxine Waters (D-CA)	82	97	90	86
"New School" Senators				
Barbara Boxer (D-CA)	88	100	94	88
Phil Gramm (R-TX)	85	99	93	84
Jesse Helms (R-NC)	71	98	88	80
James Inhofe (R-OK)	95	100	97	90
Trent Lott (R-MS)	82	98	94	86
Mitch McConnell (R-KY)	80	99	91	84
Howard Metzenbaum (D-OH)	79	93	87	79
Don Nickles (R-OK)	79	99	91	83
Rick Santorum (R-PA)	90	96	92	90
Strom Thurmond (R-SC)	15	98	79	79

Note: Data stop at 2000 for those members who were still serving in 2000.

him high praise. Indeed, some have described him as "the nastiest of the prosecutorial wild men of Capitol Hill, who use their power in pursuit of perceived wrongdoing."[29] Burton supported the Republicans on House roll calls a remarkable 93 percent of the time, with his party at 84 percent during those years.

Undoubtedly among the leading figures befitting the new school is Tom DeLay, the former GOP House majority leader from Texas. Nicknamed "The Hammer" because of his autocratic leadership style, DeLay does business with ruthless ideological fervor grounded in his pro-business, pro-Jesus, antigovernment, and antienvironment beliefs.[30] He "is well known for advancing the GOP's goals without regard for who he has to muscle to make sure his side wins."[31] This hard-hitting style resulted in several admonishments from the House Ethics Committee, in 1999 and again in 2004. DeLay's legislative style is described in the following fashion:

> If you administered truth serum to members of the House and asked
> whom they most blame for the fact that the place has become a snake
> pit, Republicans as well as Democrats would say Mr. DeLay, the former
> pest exterminator. He shakes down lobbyists, he bullies colleagues
> and, as perhaps the most powerful member on Capitol Hill, he seems
> to view his job not as enacting laws but as laying little bear traps for
> Democrats. Democrats, by Mr. DeLay's account, are never merely
> mistaken, they are unpatriotic or godless or tools of nefarious special
> interests.[32]

Upon his departure, the *USA Today* used the following words to
describe DeLay's approach to politics and his career in the House: he
frequently employed "strong-arm tactics," he was "more vindictive
than conservative," he used "power as a goal itself rather than as
means to achieve something broader for the public's benefit," and he
"sent out a message that virtually any behavior was OK so long as
it benefited the GOP."[33] DeLay voted with his party at a 92 percent
clip, with his party average at 84 percent. Not far from DeLay in
partisanship is Bob Dornan, former Republican from California,
known for his vitriolic speeches on the House floor. Dornan ranked at
83 percent for his party support, with his party at 81 percent during
his House career.

Without a doubt, the person who appears to have personified
the new school is Newt Gingrich, former GOP House speaker from
Georgia. Gingrich represented the combative, no holds barred style
of leadership. Indeed, he rose to power by being confrontational.
"Frustrated at th[e] conciliatory attitude, several more junior
House Republicans, led by Gingrich, formed the Conservative Opportunity Society (COS) in 1982, to pursue a more aggressive,
partisan strategy....Gingrich's strategy was...not only predicated on
questioning the ethics of individual Democrats but on denigrating
Congress as an institution."[34] As a backbencher in the 1980s, he
regularly attacked Democratic leaders of the time, and was perhaps
single-handedly responsible for the ouster of Jim Wright, the former
Democratic House speaker.

In *The Broken Branch*, Mann and Ornstein describe Gingrich's
strategy of leadership since the day he entered the House:

> It was based on the belief that as long as Republicans went along to get
> along, cooperating with Democrats to make the House work and focusing
> on winning seats in the House one by one, the advantages of incumbency

and the tendency of the public to hate the Congress but love their own congressman would allow the Democrats to stay in the saddle indefinitely. Republicans were going to have to nationalize the congressional election process and broaden the public hatred of Congress until enough voters became convinced that the place was thoroughly corrupt and dysfunctional and that sweeping change was necessary. Gingrich disdained the kind of majority/minority partnerships that had worked for so long on committees like Ways and Means and between Speakers and Minority Leaders. He wanted to dramatize regularly that the House was run by Democrats, had been run by Democrats for a quarter century, and that the Democrats had been corrupted by their own power.[35]

In his voting record, Gingrich stands at 84 percent for his career, while his party stood at 81 percent during those years.

In the partisan vein, Democrat David Obey of Wisconsin ranked at 88 percent, and his party at 80 percent. Nancy Pelosi, Democrat from California, is also more partisan than her party. Indeed, she acquired her leadership position due to her very partisan credentials. She supported Democratic votes on 93 percent of the issues, with her party average at 86 percent. Bob Walker, former GOP congressman from Pennsylvania, was similarly partisan, standing at 93 percent for his House career, with the GOP at 81 percent. Maxine Waters, Democrat from California, is known for her vitriol against the Republicans. She "brings to her work a fury that is almost palpable, and an insistence that she will assert herself regardless of protocol, partly perhaps a result of anger but also a weapon she uses shrewdly and cynically to get both publicity and results. 'I don't have time to be polite,' she says."[36] Waters stands at 90 percent support for Democratic positions, with the party average at 86 percent. The only person in this group who averaged lower than his party was Bob Livingston, former Republican from Louisiana, coming in at 77 percent during his career, with his party at 82 percent.

In the new Senate, every single new guard senator has supported his or her party more than the party average. In other words, each one of these senators was more partisan than their fellow Democrats or Republicans. Barbara Boxer, a California Democrat, is known as a partisan ideologue, who has shown 94 percent support for the party, with the party average at 88 percent. Former Texas Republican Phil Gramm, who was once a Democrat, displayed a sharp ideological tongue during his congressional career. He was a strong conservative by any measure. Gramm stands at 93 percent for his career average, with his party at 84 percent. Jesse Helms, former Republican of North Carolina, justifiably acquired the reputation as a right-wing ideologue, who "has gotten into confrontation with virtually every other member of the Senate."[37] Nicknamed "Senator No," Helms was "mostly in the posture of opposition" during his Senate career.[38] Fred Barnes noted in the *Weekly Standard:* "Helms follows a simple formula: Implacability equals strength. It works. He can't be buffaloed—or ignored.... The point here is Helms has gained strange, new respect not as many conservatives have—by moving left. Helms has earned it the hard way—by not moving at all."[39] Helms supported the GOP 88 percent of the time during his career, with the party average at 80 percent during those years.

Another die-hard partisan and ideologue in the Senate's new guard is James Inhofe, Republican of Oklahoma. According to a Hill observer, Inhofe "has little patience for traditional Hill decorum."[40] He is "such a self-righteous blowhard that compromise, and thus accomplishment, elude him. He is known mainly for the things he has undone."[41] Inhofe is one of the staunchest supporters of his party, standing at 97 percent for the GOP, with his party at 90 percent.

Mississippi Republican and former Senate leader Trent Lott, trained in the Gingrich school of politics in the House, also represented a more hard-nosed attitude. Chosen as the Senate majority leader in 1996, Lott was much more ideological than his predecessor, Bob Dole. According to some observers, Lott "does a better job at cajoling, intimidating, and influencing committee chairs."[42] Political scientist Thomas Mann notes: "Lott has been a very aggressive majority leader, especially in cutting off all Democratic opportunities to offer amendments. This has not only irritated Democrats but emboldened Daschle to fight fire with fire. It's not a pretty sight."[43] However, when it came to his leadership duties, Lott was also known for working generally well with Tom Daschle, his Democratic counterpart. He is "an instinctive deal-maker, not much interested in quixotic gestures, an orderly and well-organized man who is dismayed by the dilatoriness of others.... He can be sharp in debate, aggressively partisan and combative, but he is gregarious and personable, striving to keep on good terms with most other members and careful to cultivate those whose support he needs."[44] Lott averaged his support for the GOP positions at 94 percent, with his party at 86 percent.

Mitch McConnell, GOP senator from Kentucky, has also been a very aggressive and a very partisan member of the new guard. McConnell is often quick to criticize Democrats and is relentless about pushing Republican causes. His party support stands at 91 percent, considerably higher than the party average of 84 percent. Howard Metzenbaum, a fiery former Democrat from Ohio, was also known to be exceedingly more partisan than his fellow Democrats in the Senate. Metzenbaum supported his party 87 percent of the time, with the party average at 79 percent.

Don Nickles, a former Republican senator from Oklahoma, also possessed strong conservative views and was often bitterly partisan on the Senate floor, although he occasionally showed willingness to work with some Democrats. At the end of his tenure, his Senate career was summed up as follows:

> The former businessman quickly carved out a role as an obstructionist in what has become a lifelong crusade to rein in the federal government.... Despite his proven ability to kill legislation, Nickles is no "Senator No," the moniker given to his more fervently ideological former colleague, Jesse Helms, R-N.C. (1973–2003). To the contrary, Nickles is broadly regarded as a personable pragmatist who, despite his personal brand of unmitigated conservatism, has worked well with colleagues of all ideological stripes....Nickles' collegiality was on full display at the beginning of the 108th Congress, when he and Democrat Hillary Rodham Clinton of New York, a longtime opponent dating back to the administration of President Bill Clinton, worked together to extend unemployment benefits.[45]

In the end, Nickles showed more partisan stripes than his Republican colleagues in the Senate, standing at 91 percent for his support for GOP positions, with his party at 83 percent.

Former Pennsylvania Republican Rick Santorum was known for his brashness, for his lack of respect for Senate's history and traditions, and for his passionately ideological stances. Indeed, he was brash as soon as he entered the Senate. Immediately upon arriving in the Senate, Santorum took on veteran Republican Senator Mark Hatfield of Oregon. Santorum wanted his party to deny Hatfield his chairmanship of the Senate Appropriations Committee because Hatfield voted against a constitutional amendment that would have required balanced budgets. Bob Dole intervened on behalf of Hatfield, and he continued as chair of the Appropriations panel. But this incident clearly showed that Santorum had no regard for Senate's norms. The episode prompted Teresa Heinz (now Teresa Heinz Kerry), widow of former Pennsylvania GOP Senator John Heinz, to characterize

Santorum as part of a "worrisome breed" of politicians who "mock, belittle and vilify those who disagree with him."[46] Ornstein notes: "Santorum is not alone; nor is he the first brash freshman willing to challenge his elders. But his early approach to legislative compromise, and his lack of interest in his institution's history and traditions, are becoming more, rather than less common."[47] Santorum is a staunch partisan, who has supported his party 92 percent of the time, with the party average at 90 percent. Finally, Strom Thurmond, a genteel but partisan former Republican senator from South Carolina, tied with his party at 79 percent.[48]

These figures show that the new guard members are driven by partisanship, for all of them endorsed their party stands more than the average member did. Pure partisanship, as I have argued above, is not a problem by itself. What is a problem is for members to wear their partisan badges all the time and to show an unwillingness to resolve differences with the other side.

The basic point is that Congress is out of order. The legislative behavior of the new guard is substantively different from that of the old guard. The new guard is in for themselves; the old guard was in more for the institution. These days members are frequently driven to protect their own or their party's ambitions, without concerning themselves with the implications of that behavior for the institution of Congress or for the nation. Quite naturally, such behavior results in divisive politics, witnessed every day in the corridors of Congress.

This behavior, of course, leads us into the ultimate Burkean dilemma of representation: concern for the constituency or for the country. My point is that members of Congress must care a little more for the collective good rather than being solely and constantly obsessed with their personal interests. A focus on the "big picture" is all the more necessary in a legislative body, which is based upon the varied interests of all members, representing the entire nation. But the crux of the problem is larger than a question of representation. It is about an attitude.

More to the point of this chapter, the new guard lives in the houses of incivility and brashness. Members these days are quick to judge, ready to demonize their opponents. Constant campaigning makes this possible, unregulated campaign contributions make this possible, and members' attitude makes this possible. The reliance on political tactics to win small battles in the short run makes governing and institutional respect extremely untenable in the long run. There is no need to be judgmental or condescending or vitriolic.

Partisanship is important, but one need not wear the partisan badge all the time. Partisanship has indeed been on the rise since the 1970s, as party unity scores at the aggregate level often cited in political science literature clearly show. However, the evidence presented in this chapter at the individual level shows that members exhibited strong partisan tendencies prior to the 1970s also, but yielded to the bargaining table at the end of the day to cut deals and get things done. If they were partisan, they were partisan with a smile. Compromise and civility are necessary to carry the day in a diverse legislative body. The modern member must recognize that Congress is inherently incapable of functioning properly without bargaining, compromise, and mutual respect.

These are, of course, enduring questions that have plagued all democratic structures. There are no easy answers, no quick fixes. But, a change in attitude by members of Congress would go a long way toward fixing the legislative ills.

CHAPTER 4

WHAT IS BEHIND PARTISANSHIP AND UNCIVIL DEBATE IN CONGRESS?

When priests are more in word than matter;
When brewers mar their malt with water;
When nobles are their tailors' tutors;
No heretics burn'd, but wenches' suitors;
When every case in law is right;
No squire in debt, nor no poor knight;
When slanders do not live in tongues;
Nor cutpurses come not to throngs;
When usurers tell their gold i' the field;
And bawds and whores do churches build;
Then shall the realm of Albion
Come to great confusion.

William Shakespeare, *King Lear*, act 3, sc. 2, 81–92

Sometimes statesmanship isn't television combat. It's just a
clever wink and a prudent nod.

David Brooks, *New York Times*

In his farewell address to the U.S. Senate, former Senator William Cohen, Republican of Maine, remarked the following:

> Congress is an institution designed to permit ideas and interests to compete passionately for public approbation and support. It was never intended to be a rose garden where intellectual felicities could be exchanged with polite gentility. Life in politics was intended to be "a roar of bargain and battle." But enmity in recent times has become so intense that some members of Congress have resorted to shoving matches in hallways adjacent to hearing

rooms. The Russian Duma, it seems, has been slouching its way toward the Potomac as debate has yielded to diatribe. There is a dynamic force at work today that is producing a gravitational pull away from center-based politics on both the left and right. Those who seek compromise and consensus are depicted with scorn as a "mushy middle" that is weak and unprincipled. By contrast, those who plant their feet in the concrete of ideological absolutism are heralded as heroic defenders of truth, justice, and the American way.[1]

There are many variables behind the partisan and ideological warfare in American politics at present. Most of them are well known to political scientists, but perhaps not so familiar to the general public. In this chapter, I summarize the accumulated knowledge as to why there is such negative intensity in today's political debates on the Hill.

Based upon received wisdom, it appears that there are a half-dozen readily apparent reasons behind the continuing bitterness between the parties in Congress. Let me explain how each of these contributes to political madness.

Let us start with political parties. Parties in American politics have changed in crucial ways over the last fifty years. At one level, individual voters do not identify as strongly with a political party as they used to. On another level, fewer individual voters now identify with a party at all compared to previous decades. Indeed, the size of the independent voter has doubled in the past fifty years. Where in 1952 about 20 percent of the nation's population claimed to be independent; that number rose to 40 percent in 2000.[2]

Along with the growth of independent voters has come a rise in split-ticket voting in American national elections. Increasingly, voters have cast their ballots for a president of one party and for a member of Congress of the other party. In 1952, the percentage of congressional districts that voted for a president of one party and a congressional candidate of the other party was about 17 percent. That number climbed to a startling figure of over 45 percent in 1992, maintaining an upward trend from 1952 to 1992, although fluctuating from year to year. Since 1968 in particular, the percentage of split-ticket voting has rarely fallen below 30 percent.[3]

The consequence has been many years of divided government in the modern era of American politics, where one party has controlled one institution and the other party has been in charge of the other. According to political scientist Morris Fiorina, a majority of congressional and presidential elections (13 out of 20) from 1952 to 1992 produced divided governments.[4] Especially since 1968 once again, an even greater majority of national elections have resulted in divided governments. This phenomenon has real consequences for politics. As Uslaner has argued, "[s]ince 1981, divided government has contributed to the problem of incivility by adding a sharper partisan edge to the already widespread waning of Congressional norms. Democrats in the Congress and Republicans in the executive branch refuse to cooperate with each other, lest each lose face in a battle for electoral predominance."[5]

Political parties changed in another vital aspect as well. In addition to the decline in voters' loyalties to parties came the parties' own demise in organizing and running political campaigns in the latter half of the twentieth century. The parties' own weakness in orchestrating political campaigns was a major sea change, creating an opportunity for political candidates to run their own campaigns. This transformation, referred in trade lingo as the shift from "party-centered" elections to "candidate-centered" elections, made every candidate an independent operative. That meant that candidates would raise their own money, hire their own consultants and strategists, and devise their own message. Each congressional election therefore became a localized contest, without a great deal of coordination from national parties.

According to Paul Herrnson, a student of congressional elections,

> [c]andidates, not political parties, are the major focus of congressional campaigns, and candidates, not parties, bear the ultimate responsibility for election outcomes....In the United States, parties do not run congressional campaigns nor do they become the major focus of elections. Instead, candidates run their own campaigns, and parties contribute money or election services to some of them....The need to win a party nomination forces congressional candidates to assemble their own campaign organizations, formulate their own election strategies, and conduct their own campaigns. The images and issues they convey to voters in trying to win the nomination carry over to the general election.[6]

Gary Jacobson, a noted expert on congressional elections, explains the situation in the following way: "Congressional election campaigns are decidedly candidate centered. They are best understood as ventures undertaken by individual political entrepreneurs in a decentralized political marketplace."[7] He continues, "[a]lthough national parties have recently expanded their efforts to recruit and finance candidates, most serious congressional aspirants operate, out of choice or necessity, as individual political entrepreneurs. The risks, pains, and rewards of mounting a campaign are largely theirs. Most instigate their own candidacies, raise most of their own resources, and put together their own campaign organizations. Their skills, resources, and strategies have a decisive effect on election outcomes."[8]

Anthony King, a respected observer of American and British politics, puts it this way:

> The factor of party still matters in American electoral politics, but less so than anywhere else in the democratic world. As a result, American legislators seeking reelection are forced to raise their own profiles, to make their own records and to fight their own reelection campaigns. If the term "swing" captures well the relative impersonality of British electoral politics, the term "entrepreneur"—with its connotations of aggressive individualism—captures perfectly the style that...elective politicians in the United States are forced to adopt....The candidate's party is a background factor. It is the candidate himself who is in the foreground.[9]

Writing for a *Washington Post* article, David Broder, another astute observer of American politics, captured this state of affairs particularly well: "In our era of debilitated political parties, Washington is run by 536 individual political entrepreneurs—one president, 100 senators and 435 members of the House—each of whom got here essentially on his own. Each chooses the office he seeks, raises his own money, hires his own pollster and ad-maker and recruits his own volunteers. Each of them is scrambling to remain in office, no matter what. And each of them has commitments and objectives he considers paramount."[10]

The fact that candidates in House and Senate contests are essentially lone rangers undoubtedly has significant implications for American politics as well. Without the discipline of parties, office-seekers operate in a Hobbesian world of trying to make it on their own, without proper training or values, much like a child attempts to make it on his own without the structure and guidance of his parents. The instinctive reaction, without proper discipline and foresight, is to win at all costs. In such a situation, candidates behave like children, feeling free to demonize each other and essentially traversing on whatever low road is necessary to win an election. This, of course, lowers the bar, the standard of decency, in American campaigns.

At the institutional level, political parties have transformed their ways of conducting themselves over the last few decades, which add immensely to the bitter political environment. For one thing, both parties have used the redistricting process, designed to redraw congressional districts in every state every ten years based upon population shifts, to create overwhelmingly safe districts for both sides. In 1960, 58.9 percent of House incumbents were considered "safe," i.e., reelected with 60 percent or more of the two-party vote in the district. In 1970, that number rose to 77.3 percent. In 1980, it dipped just a bit to 72.9 percent. In 1990, it climbed again to 76.4 percent. In 2000, it stood at 77.3 percent.[11] In recent elections, out of 435, hardly more than two dozen seats have been competitive. In the remaining 400-plus seats, the incumbent or the party with greater registrations in the district is highly likely to carry that seat.

Most members of both parties, through the process of redrawing district lines, have essentially conspired to create secure seats for themselves, assuring very little competition for an ungodly number of seats. The redistricting process, the way it works now, essentially permits each member of Congress to select their voters rather than permitting the voters to pick their congressmen and women! As Bill Thomas, the California Republican, told Eilperin about his opposition in the 2004 reelection contest, "I had no one. That's outrageous.... You have the creation of districts that are more selected by the candidate than the constituent."[12]

As a result of such redistricting shenanigans of the past few decades, most Democratic districts are now made up of mostly Democrats, and most Republican districts now constitute mostly Republicans. That means that representatives who represent Democratic districts have no need to cater to Republican views, and the representatives who represent Republican districts have no need to cater to Democratic views. This only helps to distance the two parties, since neither side has the incentive to talk to each other, or more significantly, to listen to each other. Indeed, the districts are so heavily partisan that the more partisan the member becomes, the more he or she is liked, not just by the constituents but more importantly by other interested groups.

In *The Broken Branch*, Mann and Ornstein discuss this phenomenon in the following terms:

> This ideological sorting by party has now extended to voters, activists, and elected officials throughout the country, creating two rival teams whose internal unity and ideological polarization are deeply embedded in the

body politic. Increasing geographical segregation of voters and successive waves of incumbent-friendly redistricting have contributed to this development by helping to reduce the number of competitive House seats to a few dozen. With the overwhelming majority of House seats safe for one party or the other, new and returning members are naturally most reflective of and responsive to their primary constituencies, the only realistic locus of potential opposition, which usually are dominated by those at the ideological extreme. This phenomenon has tended to move Democrats in the House left and Republicans, right.[13]

In the Senate, however, redistricting obviously plays no role. But Mann and Ornstein contend, "the same pattern of ideological polarization of the parties is present there, albeit shaped in part by politicians moving from service in the House to the Senate. Many senators brought with them to the chamber attitudes toward Congress that were shaped by the contentious combat in the House of the late 1980s and early 1990s."[14]

Moreover, institutionally, political bitterness increasingly comes from the minority's undying urge to be the majority. Both Republicans and Democrats, whichever side happens to be in the minority, engage in the same partisan tactics in the hopes of achieving the majority status in the next election. In fact, much of political activity these days is geared by this hope. So, for example, the Democrats refuse to compromise on Social Security reform or health care reform or education reform or whatever other pet Democratic causes because the thinking is that when they are in power, they can then decide the issue on their terms. Hence, even if they might like some versions of the Republican reform proposals, the Democrats refuse to go along so as not to "give" that issue away to the GOP and allow the GOP to claim credit for solving a major problem. Likewise, the Republicans refuse to compromise with the Democrats on their pet causes, with the hope that when they are in power they will do it their way and not allow the other side to "steal" their issue.

These are among the unending saga of issues and the back-and-forth between the two parties on such issues. The hope and the desire for each side is that when we are in the majority, we will deal with the issue and claim *all* credit for it rather than sharing some of the limelight with the other side.

Another partisan transformation of recent decades that contributes significantly to the partisan divide is the tendency to choose congressional leaders, and even committee chairs in certain cases, who represent the ideological extremes of the two parties. Congressional leaders themselves no longer come from the moderate, compromising wings of the parties. In the House, after Tom Foley, the Democrats selected Richard Gephardt of Missouri and later Nancy Pelosi of California, coming not from the centrist rolls of the party. The Republicans following Bob Michel went to Newt Gingrich, then to Tom DeLay of Texas, and subsequent to DeLay's indictment in 2005, to Roy Blunt of Missouri, men not from the mainstream of the GOP. On the Senate side, the GOP leadership in recent years has not included the likes of Howard Baker or Everett Dirksen. Instead, the Republican lineup has included conservative stalwarts, ranging from Trent Lott of Mississippi to Bill Frist of Tennessee to Mitch McConnell of Kentucky. The Democrats too have abandoned the center in naming their leaders and, rather than having the likes of a Lyndon Johnson or a Mike Mansfield at the party's helm, have gone toward those with leading liberal credentials, such as Harry Reid of Nevada and Dick Durbin of Illinois.

Indeed, the test is for ideological purity, not the ability to compromise or lead with innovative ideas or produce broadly acceptable results, is what matters any more in the selection of congressional leaders. This tendency, to pick men and women who represent the staunchest elements of the party and will always tow the party line, has spilled over in the selection of committee chairmanships also, even at the cost of the seniority rule. Considered an inviolate rule from the time it was instituted in the early part of the twentieth century, the seniority rule allows the member of the majority with the longest service on the panel to become committee chair. It is intended to minimize the arbitrary influence of party leadership in the selection of committee chairs. However, in recent years the rule has been violated on several occasions, especially by the Republicans.

In 1995, Gingrich, then the newly elected speaker, assigned chairmanships of certain pivotal committees to those with less seniority, but much more party loyalty, than others on the panels. Those whom he chose were much more likely to faithfully execute the party's, hence the leadership's, agenda. His successor, Dennis Hastert of Illinois, went further, leading an effort to establish an elaborate interview process where candidates make their pitch for a committee chairmanship. "The candidates will be given an opportunity to discuss their legislative agenda, oversight agenda, how they intend to organize the committees, and their communication strategy," he wrote. In this context, fund-raising is also important. "You can't tell a Member who raises $1 million for the party and visits 50 districts is not going to have an advantage over someone who sits back and thinks he's entitled to a chairmanship. Those days are gone," said a top GOP leadership aide.[15] According to Roger Davidson and Walter Oleszek, two prominent Congress scholars, "[i]n effect, many of the criteria employed to designate GOP chairmen are comparable to those that top party leaders must possess: coalition-building skills, fund-raising ability, and talent for media advocacy. (Party loyalty is another important criterion.)"[16]

These elements show that political parties have been on the decline in the last few decades. Where parties are no longer at work, other actors, such as interest groups and political consultants, as discussed below, rapidly moved in to fill that vacuum. The partisan changes involve about a half-a-dozen different features surrounding parties, as noted above, and all of them have contributed to increasing divisiveness in Congress.

On top of the transformation of political parties at various levels, interest groups have also come to play a decisive role in the political bitterness. Indeed, observed political scientist Martin Wattenberg: "With the decline in the salience of political parties to the electorate since 1960, group identifications have become increasingly important to voters as alternative political reference points."[17] Moreover, with reference to the reconstituted activities of interest groups, he noted, "[a]s political parties have lost much of their relevance over the past several decades and hence their ability to mobilize the public, interest groups have acquired resources that have made them more powerful than ever before. Direct-mail strategies have enabled groups to organize potential members better, to communicate with them about key issues, and to raise money for campaigns."[18]

Interest groups came to prominence on the American political scene in the 1960s and 1970s. Prior to this time, the number of interest groups in American politics was quite limited. The 1960s, and especially the 1970s, saw an explosive growth in the number of interest groups. According to political scientists Kay Schlozman and John Tierney, 40 percent of interest groups were established after 1960 and 25 percent were founded after 1970.[19]

The growth in interest groups came as a consequence of a general demand in American society to open up the political system. The accusation was that the political system worked only to the benefit of the already-privileged populations of the society. The idea was that the interest groups would allow the not-so-privileged segments of the society to have a seat at the table as well. Therefore, after the mid-1970s, many interest groups were created to champion the causes of the minorities, women, the environmentalists, and so on.

However, opening up the political system meant exposing the government to increased public scrutiny. Government would no longer be where decisions were made in the proverbial "dark, smoke-filled rooms," but rather in the glare of open sunlight. Indeed, many congressional reforms of the 1970s, ranging from open committee meetings to recorded votes subject to public view to televised debates in the House and Senate, came about from this line of thinking.[20] This openness gave interest groups not only access to decision-makers, but indeed the right, according to them, to fight for their causes. As a result, in addition to advocacy for their causes, interest groups have now become confrontational in how they go about their business.

After several editions of exhaustive studies about the politics of interest groups in contemporary American politics, prominent interest groups scholars Allan Cigler and Burdett Loomis conclude with the following:

> If, as we suggest, lobbying efforts on major political issues have come increasingly to look like national electoral campaigns, replete with slick advertisements, intense and extreme rhetoric, high-tech mobilization of supporters, and the expenditure of large sums of money, the short-term implications are not positive. Such efforts contribute to the fragmentation and disintegration of our political order, without enhancing its representation or deliberative aspects. Many voices may be raised, but few are genuinely heard and evaluated in the plebiscitary environment that characterizes the debate over issues.... Because closure is so difficult to obtain, the policies that do emerge are more likely to be token than substantial and more symbolic than real, further disillusioning a citizenry already cynical and suspicious of politicians' lofty promises.[21]

Even over the long-term, Cigler and Loomis are suspicious about the benefits of public lobbying techniques to legislators. To them, interest groups primarily provide information, which may often be biased, to lawmakers to help reduce uncertainty in politics. "The many sophisticated, highly orchestrated attempts by organized interests to communicate with lawmakers run the risk of being largely discounted by policy makers already overwhelmed with information the accuracy and reliability of which is often difficult to judge....Elective politicians, a most sensitive breed, may well try to sniff out their own, independent sources of information on the political ramifications of major policy decisions."[22]

After conducting their far-ranging examination, Mark Rozell and Clyde Wilcox, two political scientists, offer a prominent perspective about the problems with the way the interest groups operate these days:

> [w]hen interest groups seek nominations for their own members, they usurp the power of parties. Whey they create advertisements to sway the larger electorate, they usurp the role not only of parties but also of the candidates themselves. When they help finance elections, they buy or "rent" members of Congress, influencing the content of legislation in ways that may be harmful to the nation as a whole. When they endorse candidates, they create misleading and oversimplified messages and distort incumbents' records, often sponsoring "attack" advertising campaigns that increase public cynicism and decrease voter turnout. Finally, when interest groups place ideological purity above all else, they undermine the pragmatic compromise that is the bedrock of American democracy.[23]

On the other hand, the argument goes, interest groups are representations of "pure democracy in action." Rozell and Wilcox themselves seem noncommittal in this debate, stating that "[i]n our view, the current and evolving role of interest groups has positive and negative implications for the conduct of American elections and for democracy more broadly."[24]

Finally, in his look at interest group activity, James Q. Wilson discusses the transition from economic to social concerns and how that makes compromises difficult:

> In the past, the major ones—the National Association of Manufacturers, the Chamber of Commerce, and labor organizations like the AFL-CIO—were concerned with their own material interests. They are still active, but the loudest messages today come from very different sources and have a very different cast to them. They are issued by groups concerned with social and cultural matters like civil rights, managing the environment, alternatives to the public schools, the role of women, access to firearms, and so forth, and they directly influence the way people view politics.[25]

He concludes, "[i]nterest groups preoccupied with material concerns can readily find ways to arrive at compromise solutions to their differences; interest groups divided by issues of rights or morality find compromise very difficult."[26]

Today, interest groups are often at the center of adversarial campaigns and adversarial political debates. Indeed, their prominence seems to increase with every passing year. Examples abound of groups taking sides on all manner of issues ranging from abortion to trade to health care to judicial nominations. They produce advertisements much like elective politicians would and raise and contribute millions of dollars for their pet causes to selected legislators. In so doing, interest groups now employ the familiar tactics of politics by using divide-and-conquer strategies and us-against-them mentality to generate rifts among people. In 2004, a new crop of groups, called "527s," labeled after the section of the Internal Revenue Service code regulating them, became active players, dividing the electorate on issues spanning from same-sex marriage to abortion to Democratic presidential nominee John Kerry's service in Vietnam.

In addition to the destructive part played by the interest groups, the dramatic growth of the media in the second half of the twentieth century also significantly contributed to political bitterness. Indeed, perhaps the single biggest factor that has exacerbated political wrangling in American politics has been the role of television. Adam Walinsky, an aide to Robert Kennedy, once observed, "Television has ruined every single thing it has touched."[27]

Television in national politics came into prominence in the late 1950s and early 1960s. The 1970s and 1980s saw an explosive growth in cable television, which brought the 24-hour news cycle, and talk radio. Indeed, C-SPAN, the Cable-Satellite Public Affairs Network, began airing proceedings in the House in 1979 and proceedings in the Senate in 1986. The 1990s saw the introduction of Internet to politics.

The introduction of television into House and Senate proceedings was based upon the rationale that it would make government transparent. Always shrouded in mystery and arcane procedures, supporters of allowing cameras into the House and Senate said that, as the people's branch, Congress should be open and accessible to the people. Opponents, however, especially in the Senate, feared that permitting C-SPAN to broadcast the floor and committee debates "would encourage its members to 'grandstand' rather than to focus on legislative business and would show the institution at its worst."[28]

Indeed, as an example, the notion of grandstanding became glaringly apparent in the events leading up to a debate on the Iraq conflict. On the eve of a debate in early 2007, Lyndsey Layton and Jonathan Weisman write, "[b]oth parties will jockey for prime time before the C-SPAN cameras, with leaders claiming the best time slots and rank-and-file members trying to make the most of the five minutes each will be allotted." They continue, "[a]lthough the order of speakers has not yet been set, Democrats and Republicans are vying for the most desired slots at a time when attention in Washington will focus on the House. Lawmakers from the West Coast do not want to speak early in the morning, when their constituents are asleep; those from the East do not want to appear at 11:25 p.m. And nearly everyone wants to talk in time to make the evening news and beat the daily newspapers' deadlines."[29]

After more than twenty years of gavel-to-gavel coverage of Congress, it appears that the introduction of television into House and Senate proceedings has done more harm than good to the institution's public image. While transparency in government functioning and decision-making is a good thing, members of both chambers and of both parties have far too often exploited the debates for political, and frequently patently partisan, purposes. Since its introduction, many members have come to the realization that television, while a curse in the sense that it opened up government proceedings to the outside world, was a blessing for pursuing political causes.

Television, specifically, gave members significant opportunities to "pose" for their particular audiences. Indeed, in the 1980s, Gingrich, then a backbencher, saw C-SPAN in the House as an opportunity to derail the Democratic leadership at the time. He constantly used "special orders" sessions, allowing members to speak about whatever they wished to speak about, often late at night, to denounce Wright, then the Democratic speaker, and others in the Democratic leadership for their ethical transgressions and other shortcomings. In so doing, he employed the politics of venom; scored political points with those, especially on the far right, who resented Democratic dominance of the House; amassed a political base of his own; and, in the end, led the GOP to the majority status in 1994. As Mann and Ornstein write:

> Gingrich's strategy was to use the new openness on the House floor, including the television coverage now provided by C-SPAN, for political advantage. Soon, dissident Republicans were offering regular floor amendments to bills designed to put Democrats in embarrassing positions whereby their votes could be used as campaign fodder; and Republicans began to take to the deserted House floor after regular business, using a procedure called "special orders," to orchestrate colloquies that bashed the majority.[30]

As a consequence, the Democrats "grew increasingly agitated at the rhetoric, often overheated and hyperbolic....Since C-SPAN cameras were usually fixed on the particular member who was speaking, it was not apparent to viewers that the chamber was largely empty. When no Democrat rose to counter or rebut the charges, it appeared as if they had no defense and that the charges were therefore true."[31]

Using the House and Senate floor to denigrate the opposition appears to have been a staple for the members of the minority party. It gives them a stage from which to vent their frustrations at the majority, otherwise unavailable to the minority, especially in the House. In recent years, many members of the minority have taken to the floor to rail against the majority leadership. Most intend to expose the highly partisan, and certainly to them, unfair behavior on the part of the majority, although speakers themselves end up resorting to highly partisan and accusatory speeches.

It is also true that once the cameras are turned on, otherwise perfectly rational and reasonable members turn into partisan warriors. Off camera, they make perfect sense, but with the cameras on, their instinctive reaction is to make partisan statements, usually designed to appeal to their political base. Liberal members make statements with liberal groups in mind; conservatives make their own statements with right-wing groups in mind. They are designed to do nothing but appeal to that political audience (the labor union groups, the gay rights groups, the tax cutting crowd, or the gun rights crowd), perhaps in the hopes of generating more political support, more campaign dollars, or more favorable media coverage. In turn, such statements only serve to alienate colleagues across the aisle and make legislating difficult.

Ronald Elving, a veteran Hill-watcher, writes:

> On balance, however, what C-SPAN has wrought is not a new Congress but a new level of public awareness of what Congress looks and sounds like. When the institution is at its best, as when it debated the resolutions to use force in the Persian Gulf in January 1991, the exposure has helped shape a favorable attitude from the public. But when it is not on its best behavior, the cameras have been telling witnesses. "C-SPAN just magnifies what's there to see," Representative Jim Leach of Iowa has said. "The warts are more evident. Spats are not perceived well by the public, and personality spats in particular do not wear well."[32]

Unfortunately, however, precisely when the cameras are on, Congress has rarely been on its best behavior.

Referring to harsh language and political wrangling one now frequently observes in congressional debates, Elving notes,

> [r]ecently, the self-wounding rhetoric has been carried over from campaigns to the House and Senate floor debates. During the House deliberation on a constitutional amendment to balance the budget, for example, Representative Bill Sarpalius, a Texas Democrat, looked into the C-SPAN lens and said, "We are all thieves." Not to be outdone, Republican Representative Dennis Hastert of Illinois said Congress was like a nursing baby: "irresponsibility on one end and no accountability on the other."

Elving asks, "Would remarks of this sort have been made under the gavel of Sam Rayburn? Probably not. But this much is certain: if such remarks had been heard on the House floor, they would not have been conveyed live and in color into millions of households nationwide."[33]

The media have always thrived on conflict! The rise in electronic media, and more significantly in the number of media outlets, meant that there would be increased competition for stories. To get the ever-smaller share of the pie for each outlet, the media became consumed with grabbing as much attention as possible and in any way possible. The simplest way for the media to grab attention was to frame every story in the form of a contest, a drama, and pull the emotional strings of the audiences. "Dog bites man," or even "man bites man," came to be the focus of each story, with emphasis on who wins and who loses.

Moreover, the 24-hour news cycle made it necessary to constantly have things to talk about. The media need a fight, need new comments all the time. If accusations are made, one cannot wait till the next day to react. One has to respond right away in this environment, or risk been seen as guilty as charged. Thus, every comment, every story, every accusation became something like a boxing match, where punches and counterpunches would constantly flow in the hope of defeating the other side.

Several noted observers have discussed how the nature of the modern media contributes to political corrosion in American politics. Todd Gitlin issues the following indictment:

> In the reasoning that grips the media market, deliberation brings no payoff; it is merely a sideshow. The media's only standards of value are arithmetic and demographic. The name of this game is nihilism. Do not reserve this term for the pornography or flesh-gouging violence that offends you. In media, nihilism is the rule, not the exception. What I mean by the nihilism that

prevails in the media is the overwhelming prevalence of a single standard for circulation: the program's marketability. Media programmers choose what is profitable—period. Intrinsic merits—intellectual, moral, aesthetic, citizenly—are of far less significance. That the nation's central communication links should be entrusted to entities that take their predominant cues from the capital markets and have no commitment to any intellectual standard is an immense obstacle to the deliberative life of democracy.[34]

In the same spirit, Mann observes: "The modern press magnifies conflict and controversy and finds irresistible the sensational aspects of personal attacks and failures. Much of the work of the press these days is devoted to revealing to the public the hidden nefarious agendas of politicians. Talk radio contributed to a coarsening of political discussion." Accordingly, to Mann, the media are engaged in "a never-ending campaign to mobilize selectively what is oftentimes a cynical and disengaged public, often involving fear-mongering and an obvious distortion of the choices facing the country."[35]

Additionally, Wilson, in referring to the mass media, remarks:

> Not only are they themselves increasingly polarized, but consumers are well aware of it and act on that awareness. Fewer people now subscribe to newspapers or watch the network evening news. Although some of this decline may be explained by a preference for entertainment over news, some undoubtedly reflects the growing conviction that the mainstream press generally does not tell the truth, or at least not the whole truth.... The news we get is not only more omnipresent, it is also more competitive and hence often more adversarial. When there were only three television networks, and radio stations were forbidden by the fairness doctrine from broadcasting controversial views, the media gravitated toward the middle of the ideological spectrum, where the large markets could be found. But now that technology has created cable news and the Internet, and now that the fairness doctrine has by and large been repealed, many media outlets find their markets at the ideological extremes.[36]

Wilson concludes, "[t]he result is that, through commercial as well as ideological self-interest, the media contribute heavily to polarization. Broadcasters are eager for stories to fill their round-the-clock schedules, and at the same time reluctant to trust the government as a source for those stories. Many media outlets are clearly liberal in their orientation; with the arrival of Fox News and the growth of talk radio, many are now just as clearly conservative."[37]

Finally, as Fiorina writes, "[c]onflict, of course, is high in news value. Disagreement, division, polarization, battles, and war make better copy than agreement, consensus, moderation, cooperation, and peace."[38] Indeed!

With the increasing use of Internet, it became all the more easier for anyone to say anything against anyone without facts or substance. In the 2004 campaign, a new feature called "Weblogs," short for Webpages and blogs, permitted anyone to post anything on the Internet, without any standards or checks concerning the veracity of the material. If someone wanted to level a charge against someone, it became all the more easier to do so.

In addition to the explosion of interest groups and the electronic media in the political process came the rise of political consultants and pollsters. Writes Klein, "[m]ost politicians tend to be cautious, straitlaced people. Confronted by the raging television torrent, by the strange new theatrics of public performance which transformed every last word or handshake into a potentially career-threatening experience, they sought creative help to navigate the waters. And so, the pollster-consultant industrial complex was born."[39]

Pollsters and consultants make their living based upon instant analysis and instant gratification. Their focus tends to be on what to do to win today, how to keep or get my congressman or senator ahead in the game, rather than on what would be good for the nation or what might be best in the long-run. Members of Congress have increasingly employed the services of consultants and pollsters to discover the pulse of public opinion, what makes a congressman or senator popular or unpopular, devise campaign strategies and write speeches based upon that, and go for the short-term gain rather than long-term satisfaction.

Herrnson writes that most modern campaigns are conducted by "highly specialized, professional organizations." He continues, "[p]olling, mass media advertising, and direct mail are three specialized aspects of campaigning that are handled primarily by political consultants hired on a contractual basis."[40] He adds, "[p]olitical consulting has become highly professional, replete with its own standards, professional associations, and trade magazines. Consultants help budding politicians learn what to expect and what will be expected of them during the campaign. Consultants' opinions of what is strategically and tactically advisable and ethical have a major impact on candidate conduct."[41]

Larry Sabato, also a political scientist, is much more specific in defining the job of a consultant. He defines a political consultant as a "campaign professional who is engaged primarily in the provision of advice and services (such as polling, media creation and production, and direct-mail fundraising) to candidates, their campaigns, and other political committees."[42] He continues, "[w]hatever the degree of their electoral influence, consultants...have talent and enormous experience." He adds,

> [b]y and large,...consultants are hard-working professionals: very bright and capable, politically shrewd and calculating, and impressively articulate. They travel tens of thousands of miles every year, work on campaigns in a dozen or more states simultaneously, and eat, breathe, and live politics. They are no less political junkies than the candidates they serve. For the most part, they are even less concerned with issues, the parties, and the substance of politics than their clients. They are businessmen, not ideologues.[43]

Sabato, however, issues a vivid indictment of consultants. According to him:

> [t]here is no more significant change in the conduct of campaigns than the consultant's recent rise to prominence, if not preeminence, during the election season. Political consultants, answerable only to their client-candidates and independent of the political parties, have inflicted severe damage upon the party system and masterminded the modern triumph of personality cults over party politics in the United States....Consultants and the new campaign technology have not changed the essence of politics. Politics is still persuasion, still a firm, friendly handshake. But the media of persuasion are no longer the same, and the handshake may be a projection or even an illusion....What consultants seem to forget is that their work cannot be evaluated solely within the context of their profession. "Is this artful media?" or "Is this an effective piece of direct mail?" or "Did this action by a political consultant help to elect candidate X?" are legitimate questions and necessary ones for any judgment of a particular candidate's worth. But the ultimate standard by which the *profession* of political consulting is judged cannot merely be success in electing or defeating candidates. There are much more vital considerations of ethics and democracy to ponder....As the influence of consultants has grown, some very disquieting questions have begun to loom large. Influence peddling, all kinds of financial misconduct, shameful acts of deception and trickery, and improprieties with former clients who are in public office are only a few of the compromising and

unethical practices found in far too many consultants' portfolios. At the root of some of the worst offenses is a profit motive unrestrained by ties to party, ideology, or ideals. . . . As distressing as they are, the ethical concerns fade by comparison to the democratic effects wrought by consultants. Political professionals and their techniques have helped homogenize American politics, added significantly to campaign costs, lengthened campaigns, and narrowed the focus of elections. Consultants have emphasized personality and gimmickry over issues, often exploiting emotional and negative themes rather than encouraging rational discussion. They have sought candidates who fit their technologies more than the requirements of office and have given an extra boost to candidates who are more skilled at electioneering than governing. They have encouraged candidates' own worst instincts to blow with the prevailing winds of public opinion. (emphasis in original)[44]

The rise of consultants, Sabato notes, is a further consequence of the decline of political parties and the subsequent opening up of the political process.

Others have gone even further in leveling accusations at political consultants. Mike Barnicle, a former *Boston Globe* columnist, wrote a stinging condemnation:

There is no lower form of life than these political consultants who make substantial sums preparing TV commercials that lower the public dialogue to food-chain level as they try to get us to respond to our darkest and most selfish emotions. . . . Politics has never been more despicable. It has been robbed of joy, life, spontaneity, fun, wit and original thought by a larcenous joint venture of consultants and candidates who use the media . . . to persuade us that nothing is any good and everyone is lousy so we might as well vote against something or someone rather than for an issue or an individual.[45]

He further claims that consultants are "greedy morons who employ the airwaves to lie, deceive, twist, maim and loot reality."[46] Indeed, Barnicle calls for banning consultants in campaigns.

While generally defending political consultants, political scientist Stephen Medvic also blames consultants for one thing. He writes, "[i]ndeed, accountability plays a central role in virtually all models of democracy, and elections are the primary medium through which public officials are held accountable to the citizenry." He continues, "[y]et consultants appear to escape accountability. They are responsible to their clients, who in turn must answer to the people, but such indirect accountability is weak at best. In fact, recent examples of consultant malfeasance prove that voters are unwilling (or, in some ways, unable) to hold candidates accountable for what their handlers do. As a result, consultants are given a free hand to push the envelope of ethical campaign behavior."[47]

Of course, politicians now employ the services of consultants and pollsters not just as political candidates, during the campaigning process, but also as officeholders, during the governing process. This has increasingly blurred the lines between campaigning and governing, so that the techniques that are used to campaign are now used to govern, making the governing process unnecessarily combative and difficult. As Hugh Heclo, a noted political scientist, points out, campaigning and governing must be kept separate because the former focuses on combat and conquest, whereas the latter can only be properly executed via compromise and deliberation. If the two are mixed, the consequence is a "permanent campaign," where everything is done to achieve high popularity levels, and that end justifies all means.[48]

Another variable that has contributed, indeed quite monumentally so, to political bitterness, as alluded to in the opening pages of this book, is the infusion of contentious social issues in the political process since the 1970s. According to traditional thinking, the purpose of government is to focus on national security and economic affairs, to keep the nation secure from foreign threats, to control inflation and unemployment, to look after the downtrodden, to make sure there is law and order in society, and to ensure fundamental liberties. Indeed, both Republicans and Democrats, up until recently, believed these to be the ends of government. Such sentiments are articulately reflected in the previous chapter in statements by former senators Rudman and Danforth, who entered politics and spent much of their lives in politics talking not about abortion and gay marriage but rather about national and economic security.

Beginning in the 1970s, social issues entered the political arena. In 1973, the Supreme Court handed down a landmark decision in *Roe v. Wade,* which legalized abortion. Ever since then, social issues of one kind or another, ranging frequently from abortion to capital punishment to flag burning to euthanasia to gay marriage have come to dominate debate and discussion in American politics. Indeed, as time has progressed, social issues have increasingly been placed on the front-burner of campaigns and elections, whereas economic issues have been relegated to the back seat. In almost every congressional election and campaign these days, the talk is less about traditional economic matters, the bread-and-butter issues of jobs and inflation or education and health care. Instead, recent congressional elections have shown that these matters often tend to be overshadowed by questions of whether or not someone can own a gun or whether or not someone can die the way he or she prefers or who should marry whom.

The thing about social issues is that they very easily can be, and often very easily are, used to exploit politics. Social issues tend to be about emotions, whereas economic issues tend to be more about logic. Social issues can be used to pull the emotional strings, to extract gut reactions, to instill fear in people's minds. In campaigns and elections, voters are not asked to rationally evaluate the merits of the issue. Rather, candidates, prodded by political consultants, sensationalize the issues and go directly to the people's emotions. Voters are not called upon to think carefully about the causes and consequences, but rather simply to pull the lever one way or the other. For example, there are many shades of gray in the abortion debate, but the issue often gets presented in stark black-and-white terms. The question readily is either how heartless can you be about killing an unborn baby? Or does a woman not have an unconditional right to choose? Many other questions that range in the middle frequently get ignored.

The thing about social issues also is that, with extreme ease and simplicity, they are frequently used as "wedge" issues to divide the electorate, to create "us versus them" mentality. In so doing, such issues get used to vilify one's opponents and charged, willy-nilly, of being un-American or unpatriotic or uncaring or unloving or ungodly. This is tantamount to being the most awful person on earth! If one supports the woman's right to choose in the abortion debate, one is accused of being uncaring. If one supports a person's choice to burn the flag, one is accused of being unpatriotic. If one engages in homosexual behavior or attempts same-sex marriage, one is accused of being ungodly.

As a result, the infusion of social issues makes political debate extremely untidy and easily uncivil. Charges and countercharges fly because no one, in a fast world, has the time to stop and think about where the accusations are coming from and whether or not there are merits to the charges. In the same spirit, candidates and interest groups spend millions of dollars on meaningless and baseless advertisements, political consultants anxiously struggle to advice their clients about how to "position" themselves to have an upper hand in the debate, and candidates are simply eager to win the next election.

The predominance of social issues in politics thus makes for debate that is based simply upon pulling the emotional heartstrings, upon name-calling and finger-pointing, and upon sensation rather than substance. The division of people into "for or against" camps distances Democrats from Republicans, liberals from conservatives. Indeed, the division even creates hatred for the other side. How can you possibly not oppose abortion? How can you possibly support same-sex marriage? How can you possibly not want this person to be executed?

Last but not least, a variable of enormous consequence that has also contributed to the dearth of proper civil dialogue in American politics is that there is almost no social interaction between Republicans and Democrats on the Hill these days. Most members of the two parties do not interact with each other socially, do not know each other on a social basis. This is a stark contrast to the social environment of the 1950s and 1960s.

During the 1950s, one heard famously about President Dwight Eisenhower's friendly relationships with Democratic leaders of the time. Indeed, there was mutual respect. According to Wright, former House speaker, "Mr. Rayburn never uttered a word of personal depreciation about Mr. Eisenhower. He never permitted in his presence any personal disparagement of Republican leader Joe Martin."[49] During the 1960s, one heard repeatedly about President Lyndon Johnson's associations with Republicans on the Hill. As a matter of fact, as recently as the early 1980s, one heard about the generally warm, working relationship between President Ronald Reagan and Tip O'Neill, then Democratic Speaker of the House. Recalls Martin Frost, former Texas Democrat and a member of the House Democratic leadership, "Reagan was 'comfortable working with Democrats, and he had very good people on his staff on a very high level who were willing to engage Democrats.'"[50] Bob Michel, former Republican House leader, observed that "he used to join the late Speaker Tip O'Neill for a drink after work, or play golf with Democrats on the weekend."[51]

In an article, David Broder conveys a telling story involving O'Neill and Reagan. After the assassination attempt on the former president in 1981, Max Friedersdorf, an aide to the president, recalls that O'Neill was "the first person to be admitted" into the president's room at the hospital. According to Friedersdorf, "Tip got down on his knees next to the bed, and said a prayer for the president.... The speaker stayed there quite a while. They never talked too much. I just heard him say the prayer, then I heard him say, 'God bless you, Mr. President, we're all praying for you.' The Speaker was crying. The president...was obviously sedated, but I think he knew it was the speaker because he said, 'I appreciate your coming down, Tip.'" When asked why O'Neill was the first guest, Friedersdorf said, "Well, Tip was third in line of succession...and the fact he was a Democrat didn't bother anybody. We didn't even think about it. Tip had been calling constantly to see how the president was doing. And there was a bond there." He added, "I remember the first dinner the Reagans had in the private residence was for Tip and his wife, and my wife and I were there. Tip and the president had a drink or two and started swapping Irish stories. Often, after that, Tip would say pretty harsh things about some of our legislative proposals, and the staff would want Reagan to answer him. But they trusted each other, and the president would say, 'That's just Tip,' and let it go." Asked if the same kind of relationship could happen now between a Republican president and a Democratic leader on the Hill, Friedersdorf flatly responded, "Absolutely not."[52]

Likewise, recalls Ray LaHood, former Republican congressman from Illinois, about old relationships on the Hill: "I worked for Bob Michel,...always in the minority. He worked with three speakers: Tip O'Neill, Jim Wright, and Tom Foley. There was never a cross word between them, and they worked very well together." Indeed, he says, "President Reagan's programs were passed because Bob Michel was able to reach across the aisle to talk to two different Speakers, and talk to Democrats, and persuade them....It was bipartisan. So it can be done."[53]

These days, however, it is almost unheard of for Democrats and Republicans to have lunch with each other, to socialize with a drink, or to associate with each other's families. The interaction these days between the members of the two parties is extremely limited for one thing, and the extent to which there is any interaction, it is limited to business talk. Members of the two parties, or more likely their staffs, might discuss cosponsorship of legislation or potential amendments to bills or possible concerns about issues if they serve on the same committees or represent similar constituencies. But not much beyond that, certainly not by members.

According to one observer, "[t]he lack of face time is often cited as a major reason Republicans and Democrats can't get along."[54] According to John Cochran, a veteran Congress watcher:

> the House has become faster-paced and more impersonal. It is harder than ever for lawmakers to develop the genuine friendships that can help bridge

partisan divisions. Members fly back to their districts regularly, sometimes spending less than 60 hours a week in Washington. When they are in the Capitol, fewer members socialize regularly with their colleagues. Where lawmakers once learned about bills directly from one another, these days they usually send their aides to do the talking....Relations between the top leaders have also been strained....Today, both Hastert and Pelosi say they do, indeed, value civility and want good communication....But they do not actually talk to each other regularly, one on one. "Mrs. Pelosi tends to write letters," Hastert said. "And if that's how she wants to communicate, that's fine with me. We write letters back." Most members once moved their families to Washington. That is rarer today, and it means lawmakers have few chances to get to know each other socially—the grease that once helped make the House run more smoothly....Congressional spouses once gathered to commiserate about life in Washington. "Now wives will be as cantankerous as members, because all they've heard are bad things about the other side," Rangel said [referring to Charles B. Rangel of New York, a senior House Democrat]. And life just moves faster on the Hill today. Boehlert [referring to Sherwood Boehlert, Republican of New York] pointed to electronic voting as an example. In days past, a clerk called the roll—as is still done in the Senate—which kept members milling on the floor for as long as 40 minutes, and there was time then to talk about legislation, or even baseball and children. Now, votes are sometimes conducted in as few as five minutes.[55]

It is in response to a lack of social interaction but also to understand and appreciate the history and norms of the U.S. Congress that LaHood, former Illinois Republican, David Skaggs, former Democratic congressman from Colorado, Amo Houghton, former New York Republican, and Tom Sawyer, former Ohio Democrat, began to arrange family retreats where members could socialize with each other. But, after four retreats, the interest waned. In the same spirit, in early 2005, Steve Israel, a House Democrat from New York, and Tim Johnson, a House Republican from Illinois, cofounded the Center Aisle Caucus in an effort to improve the relationships between the two parties.[56] The problem of scarcity of cross-party interaction continues to persist, however, as these efforts indicate.

As a result, most members have no knowledge of any personal characteristics of their colleagues on the other side of the aisle, their likes and dislikes, their hopes and fears, their children and grandchildren. Business talk is just that; it is professional, not personal; it is based upon legalistic agreements, not friendships; it ends when the deal ends, it does not continue indefinitely. There is no trust involved, there is no stake involved in other human beings, as it would be in friendships or other personal relationships. Fewer friendships with others mean that the other person is not to be trusted. If the person is of the other party, he or she is to be viewed with suspicion, he or she is to be constantly checked.

The consequences of lack of social interaction undoubtedly spill into the legislative process, where deals with members of the other side become difficult to make because one does not trust one another. So, the work of Congress, which is based upon cutting deals, becomes sterile and rigid and suspicious.

———

In this chapter, I have highlighted the changing roles of political parties and interest groups, the new forms of media, the emergence of political consultants, the use of contentious issues, and the lack of social interaction among members of Congress in modern American politics. I have sought to demonstrate how the reconstituted forms of these various elements have generated, contributed to, or otherwise enhanced the divisiveness and incivility in the life of contemporary politics. This chapter has simply been a synopsis, a broad overview, of these variables and their contributions to political cantankerousness on the Hill.

There are, no doubt, other, smaller elements that have also contributed to political divisions in congressional politics. But these remain the leading variables. There is also no doubt that much more details and many more scholarly studies can be added to further augment the arguments noted in this chapter. My intention, however, is not to belabor the point but simply to adequately outline the leading causes.

CHAPTER 5

WHITHER CONFIDENCE AND RESPECT IN THE MODERN CONGRESS?

The thorny point
Of bare distress hath ta'en from me the show
Of smooth civility: yet am I inland bred
And know some nurture.

Your gentleness shall force
More than your force move us to gentleness.

William Shakespeare, *As You Like It*, act 2,
sc. 7, 94–97, 102–3

Politics is a dirty word to some. But where there is no
democracy, there is no politics—and vice versa.

Alan Simpson, former Republican
senator from Wyoming

Toward the end of his farewell remarks, J. James Exon, former Democratic senator from Nebraska, said:

> The last point I would like to emphasize is that our political process must be "re-civilized." What I have called the "ever-increasing vicious polarization of the electorate, the us-against-them mentality," has all but swept aside the former preponderance of reasonable discussion of the pros and cons of many legitimate issues. Unfortunately, the traditional art of workable compromise for the ultimate good of the nation, heretofore the essence of democracy, is demonstrably eroded....The hate level, principally fed by television and radio attack ads, has unfortunately become the measurement of a successful political campaign. Much to the detriment of our nation, the political season no longer ends on Election Day. In fact, lately, it never ends....The national political structure of the United States of America has turned into one long campaign. Because of a lack of

campaign-finance reform, fund-raising is never-ending....When politics and fund-raising dominate so many of the activities of national officehold-ers, no wonder bipartisanship often falls by the wayside. No wonder the electorate becomes confused and discontented.[1]

This chapter is about the consequences of political polarization. So far in this book, I have discussed the factors that have contributed to increased polarization in American politics in recent times and high-lighted why lack of civility conflicts with debate in an open society. The next questions, then, are: What has partisanship produced? What have heightened incivility and bickering wrought?

A glaring consequence, one that cannot be taken lightly in a democratic society, is the decrease in popular regard for the legislative branch, the symbol of this nation's democracy. The drop in public esteem for Congress should be a major concern for everyone, for the people's branch acquires a tarnished image. No doubt Congress has often been the subject of popular jokes, but there is no need for members themselves, those who work there, to deliberately worsen that image. The public and members should want Congress to be held in high esteem, as it represents the American system and its principles.

The express objective of this chapter is to show the decline in public's confidence and respect for members and the institution as a result of the rise in incivility and partisanship. The two are closely linked, for increased bitterness and name-calling engender lower confidence in and respect for Congress. The chapter will show how the two parties have become increasingly coherent internally (homogeneous) and increasingly removed from each other (more and more distant ideo-logically) and how these phenomena are connected to the public's con-comitant lack of confidence in Congress and respect for its members.

In his seminal book titled *Why Americans Hate Politics*, popular journalist and political commentator E.J. Dionne, Jr., adroitly puts forward the empirical argument regarding the impact of polarization on American politics. He writes:

> Most of the problems of our political life can be traced to the failure of the dominant ideologies of American politics, liberalism and conservatism. The central argument of this book is that liberalism and conservatism are framing political issues as a series of false choices. Wracked by contradiction and responsive mainly to the needs of their various constituencies,

liberalism and conservatism *prevent* the nation from settling the questions that most trouble it. On issue after issue, there is consensus on where the country should move or at least on what we should be arguing about; liberalism and conservatism make it impossible for that consensus to express itself. (emphasis in original)[2]

Dionne continues:

The false choices posed by liberalism and conservatism make it extremely difficult for the perfectly obvious preferences of the American people to express themselves in our politics. We are encouraging an "either/or" politics based on ideological preconceptions rather than a "both/and" politics based on ideas that broadly unite us.

To be sure, free elections in a two-party system inevitably encourage polarization; voters who like some things about liberals or Democrats and some things about conservatives or Republicans end up having to choose one package or the other. In free elections, each side will always try to polarize the electorate in a way that will leave a majority standing on its side. But if free elections leave so many in the electorate dissatisfied with where they have to stand, and push large numbers out of the electorate entirely, then it is fair to conclude that the political process is badly defective.

Moreover, after the election is over, parties have to govern. But putting such a premium on false choices and artificial polarization, our electoral process is making it harder and harder for electoral winners to produce what they were elected for: good government. The false polarization that may be inevitable at election time is carrying over into the policy debates that take place afterward.[3]

He further continues his analysis:

Americans hate politics as it is now practiced because we have lost all sense of the public good. Over the last thirty years of political polarization, politics has stopped being a deliberative process through which people resolved disputes, found remedies and moved forward. When Americans watch politics now, in thirty-second snatches or even in more satisfactory formats like "Nightline" or "The MacNeil/Lehrer News Hour," they understand instinctively that politics these days is not about finding solutions. It is about discovering postures that offer short-term political benefits. We give the game away when we talk about "issues," not "problems." Problems are solved; issues are merely what politicians use to divide the citizenry and advance themselves.[4]

Dionne concludes: "This, then, is the legacy of the last thirty years: a polarized politics that highlights symbolic issues, short-circuits genuine political debate, gives discontent few real outlets, allows money a paramount role in the electoral process, and leaves the country alarmed over whether it can maintain its standard of living. Is it any wonder that Americans have come to hate politics?"[5]

As one can see, Dionne is clearly frustrated about the way politics work these days. The public watches partisan debates, prepackaged and divisive and bitter and all, and learns almost nothing about the matters at hand. Each side has pretested the messages and each side vehemently sticks to all its partisan lines, and everyone except the hard-core believers get turned off and begin to resent the system.

Noted political scientist Lawrence Dodd has also analyzed Congress in recent decades and discussed at length its inability to solve contemporary problems. According to Dodd, the increasingly self-interested and partisan nature of legislators must bear much of the blame. He writes:

> The source of policy immobilism in American politics, I suggest, lies embedded in the character of contemporary legislative politics. More so than at any other time in the nation's history, Congress is elected and organized to serve the disparate elements of a self-interested public rather than to identify and foster the shared concerns of a public-spirited citizenry. Congress increasingly lacks the ability to recognize the mutual concerns and shared interests of the public and the ability to discover new governing principles that could resolve our policy dilemmas and renew public faith in government. This magnified politics of self-interest came to predominance with the creation of the service state during the advanced industrialism of the twentieth century. In its wake has come a Congress bereft of its representative and deliberative capacities and virtually unable to acknowledge or address the new governing demands of a postindustrial society.[6]

Dodd continues:

> The problem-solving capacities of the modern Congress *are* eroding. Historically, Congress has recognized and addressed the central policy problems of the day, and thereby has sustained its popular support, through reasonably faithful representation and deliberative consideration of the public's general policy concerns. As long as Congress reflected

the major policy issues troubling the public and sought to reconcile disagreement through reasoned discussion, the public could forgive the institution's shortcomings and support its continued policymaking power. But what the citizens cannot forgive is a breakdown in the representative and deliberative consideration of the general policy concerns; when that happens the institution loses touch with the people's real-life problems and with the real-life issues that a solution to their problems must address. Yet this is precisely what has happened in contemporary America. (emphasis in original)[7]

He concludes this line of argument by noting that:

[t]he public's loss of faith in Congress may reflect an astute reading on the part of citizens that however well Congress manages the service state and addresses their immediate narrow interests, it is not attentive to the general issues shaping their collective well-being or their long-term future. In the first half of the nineteenth century Congress at least recognized the problems associated with slavery and deliberated their resolution in great debates. In the late nineteenth and early twentieth centuries Congress at least recognized the worst abuses of early industrialization and sought to regulate them. In the midtwentieth century Congress at least recognized the emerging service needs of an advanced industrial nation and created a bureaucracy to address the most basic public concerns. But as the nation enters the postindustrial era of the twenty-first century, Congress seems oblivious to the limits of the service state as a viable governing approach and to the consequent need for a re-creation of government.[8]

According to Dodd's evaluation, Congress is mired in the short-term partisan gains at the expense of solving long-term problems of the country. Each side wants that partisan edge, that fight to win just the next election, which often results in the public's loss of faith in their representatives.

Harvard University political scientist David King directly connects the problems of polarization to the issue of mistrust. The two are joined at the hip. King writes: "both political parties have been growing more extreme over the past three decades, and it is unlikely that postelection promises of bipartisanship will quickly reverse historic trends. Furthermore, the public's mistrust of government is unlikely to be reversed unless and until politicians and their parties stage a concerted return to the sensible center. The politics of polarization *is* the politics of mistrust." (emphasis in original)[9]

He continues:

> The demise of the New Deal coalition, the rise of the Republican party in the South, the declining fidelity to party labels, and the rising partisanship among political elites in Congress all point to a growing gap between the interests of political elites and the preferences of average Americans. That growing gap is being filled not by third parties—because our electoral system is profoundly hostile to third parties. The growing gap between elites and the rest of us is being filled with cynicism, mistrust, and frustration that our leaders do not care about "our" problems. One way out of this downward spiral may be for candidates, chastened by the prospect of electoral defeat, to adopt more centrist policies. This is especially difficult, however, when the parties are dominated by activists who are too often willing to sacrifice votes for the sake of ideological purity. Faced with such stark choices, voters may find mistrust to be a perfectly reasonable response.[10]

King concludes his assessment with the following:

> Inflexible partisanship is corrosive within electorates and legislatures. Of course parties play a crucial role in democracies as political intermediaries, and we want them to be responsible by announcing proposals and then delivering on them. The art of politics, however, is the art of compromise, and strange-bedfellows coalitions tend to make better laws (easier to implement, more widely supported, and more likely to stand constitutional tests) than strict and homogeneous party coalitions. This is especially important in policy areas with highly heterogeneous constituents and interests. Partisanship is too often a barrier to strange-bedfellows coalitions, and bipartisan alliances have dwindled in Congress since the mid-1970s. With our legislatures increasingly dominated by loyalists drawn from extreme elements in their own parties, legislators are inclined to inveigh against rivals. Is it any wonder why survey respondents accord politicians less respect when politicians are showing less respect among themselves?[11]

The issue of respect, thus, is central to the problem of political polarization. Politicians get less respect because they behave in ways that do not inspire confidence in the general public. Both sides prey on fear and negativity rather than instilling courage and possibilities.

The lack of confidence in and respect for Congress and its members is thus a principle result of increased partisan polarization. Greater partisanship begets greater mistrust, lowering the Congress's esteem in the eyes of the public even more. That has been the central proposition of the foregoing arguments. Let us see if the data bear out this relationship.

In his commentaries on the contemporary nature of Congress and American politics, former Congressman Hamilton makes the following claim: "The perception of Congress as paralyzed by its own internal bickering comes up in most discussions of the institution, and it is one that matters. Surveys show it is a major factor in the American public's lack of confidence in Congress."[12] This statement reflects precisely the thinking outlined above. Certainly, the anecdotal talk disdains the U.S. Congress in a highly partisan mode, but does that stand up in scientific data as well?

The empirical evidence to back up this claim and the arguments forwarded in the preceding section in this chapter is abundantly clear. In this section, I show data about increases in partisanship in Congress and the resulting lack of confidence in the institution. The basic hypothesis is that as the bitterness and the divide between the two parties increase, the public's confidence in Congress declines. The expectation, as a result, is for an inverse relationship between these two features, and the data clearly reveal that relationship.

The data regarding the increased frequency of party unity votes (i.e., votes upon which both parties' leaders seek unity, also known as partisan roll calls) are presented in Table 5.1. I shall take a few data points to show the inverse relationship. Lower party unity votes mean less partisanship; higher party unity votes mean more partisanship. For instance, in 1966, where confidence data begin, both parties in the House sought unity on 41 percent of the votes. In the Senate during the same year, both parties pressed for unity on 50 percent of the votes. The data show that public confidence in Congress during that year was at 42 percent, a remarkably high figure by today's standards.

In 1984, party unity votes in the House occurred on 47 percent of roll calls, whereas in the Senate, they took place on 40 percent of roll calls. In that year, public's confidence in Congress stood at 28 percent, a high number still by today's standards. Just a few years later, in 1987, party unity votes in the House rose to 64 percent of all roll calls, and stood at 41 percent in the Senate. During that year, public's confidence in the institution rested at 20 percent.

The party unity votes then begin to rise fairly consistently and the public's esteem of Congress begins to be ranked consistently low. In 1993, for example, House party unity votes stood at 66 percent;

Table 5.1
Party Unity Votes and Confidence in the Modern Congress

Year	House Party Unity Votes	Senate Party Unity Votes	Confidence in Congress
1966	41	50	42
1967	36	35	–
1968	35	32	–
1969	31	36	–
1970	27	35	–
1971	38	42	19
1972	27	37	21
1973	42	40	–
1974	29	44	18
1975	48	48	13
1976	36	37	9
1977	42	42	17
1978	33	45	10
1979	47	47	18
1980	38	46	18
1981	37	48	16
1982	36	43	13
1983	56	44	20
1984	47	40	28
1985	61	50	16
1986	57	52	21
1987	64	41	20
1988	47	43	15
1989	56	35	16
1990	49	54	14
1991	55	49	9
1992	65	53	16
1993	66	67	12
1994	62	52	8
1995	73	69	10
1996	56	62	10
1997	50	50	11
1998	56	56	12
1999	47	63	12
2000	43	49	15
2001	40	55	18
2002	43	46	22
2003	52	67	20
2004	47	52	13
2005	49	63	16
2006	55	57	10

Note: Party unity votes data taken from *Congressional Quarterly Weekly Report,* January 1, 2007, 39; confidence data taken from The Harris Poll, March 1, 2007.

the same measure for the Senate stood at 67 percent. In turn, the public's confidence stood at only 12 percent. In 1994, House party unity votes were at 62 percent; Senate party unity votes were at 52 percent. The confidence number during that year dropped to a mere 8 percent, an all-time low. In 1995, party unity votes in both the House and the Senate reached their highest marks in recent history. In the House, the number reached 73 percent, and in the Senate, it reached 69 percent. In response, public regard for the institution stood at 10 percent in that year. Indeed, over the last nearly twenty years, public's regard for Congress has often been in the low teens, a pitiful number for confidence in the nation's democratic symbol.

All in all, Table 5.1 shows a reasonably steady rise in party unity votes in the modern Congress and a reasonably steady concurrent drop in public's confidence in the institution. The public dislikes heightened partisanship, and shows it in its evaluation of the institution.

Table 5.2 presents data that show the extent to which members of both parties voted with their respective parties (i.e., conceded to their leaders' and parties' call for party unity). Once again, the data on both measures begin in 1966. In that year, House Democrats voted with their party 62 percent of the times, and House Republicans voted with their party 68 percent of the times. Senate Democrats voted with their party 57 percent of the times, and Senate Republicans voted with their party 63 percent of the times. Those are relatively modest averages by today's standards. Confidence in Congress in that year stood at 42 percent, a high number.

As can be seen in Table 5.2, throughout the 1970s and 1980s, the party unity scores for both parties continue to average in the 60s and 70s range, inching ever higher toward the 80s at the end of the 1980s. The confidence data, on the other hand, continue to drop. The confidence figure drops to as low as 9 percent in 1976, rises a bit in the mid-1980s, but then slumps back down to the teens by the end of the 1980s.

Then, move to 1993. In that year, party unity for both Democrats and Republicans in both the House and the Senate reached firmly into the 80 percent range for the first time in recent memory. For the House Democrats, party unity averages stood at 85 percent; for the House Republicans, they stood at 84 percent. In the other body, party unity for Democrats was at 85 percent also, and for Republicans, it was at 84 percent. The public's esteem for Congress, in turn, stood at a mere 12 percent.

As party unity within both parties in both chambers continued to register into the 80s during the 1990s, the public's regard for Congress

Table 5.2
Party Unity Scores and Confidence in the Modern Congress

Year	House Democratic Average	House Republican Average	Senate Democratic Average	Senate Republican Average	Confidence in Congress
1966	62	68	57	63	42
1967	67	74	61	60	–
1968	59	64	51	60	–
1969	61	62	63	63	–
1970	58	60	55	56	–
1971	61	67	64	63	19
1972	58	66	57	61	21
1973	68	68	69	64	–
1974	62	63	63	59	18
1975	69	72	68	64	13
1976	66	67	62	61	9
1977	68	71	63	66	17
1978	63	69	66	59	10
1979	69	73	68	66	18
1980	69	71	64	65	18
1981	69	74	71	81	16
1982	72	69	72	76	13
1983	76	74	71	74	20
1984	74	71	68	78	28
1985	80	75	75	76	16
1986	79	70	72	76	21
1987	81	74	81	75	20
1988	80	74	78	68	15
1989	81	72	78	78	16
1990	81	74	80	75	14
1991	81	77	80	81	9
1992	79	79	77	79	16
1993	85	84	85	84	12
1994	83	84	84	79	8
1995	80	91	81	89	10
1996	80	87	84	89	10
1997	82	88	85	87	11
1998	82	86	87	86	12
1999	83	86	89	88	12
2000	82	88	88	89	15
2001	83	91	89	88	18
2002	86	90	83	84	22
2003	87	91	85	94	20
2004	86	88	83	90	13
2005	88	90	88	88	16
2006	86	88	86	86	10

Note: Party unity scores data taken from *Congressional Quarterly Weekly Report,* January 1, 2007, 39; confidence data taken from The Harris Poll, March 1, 2007.

reached single-digits or barely touched double digits. In 1994, for instance, Democrats in the House voted with their party 83 percent of the times; Republicans in the House voted with their party 84 percent of the times. Democrats in the Senate voted with their fellow Democrats 84 percent of the times; Republicans in the Senate voted with their fellow Republicans 79 percent of the times, just shy of the 80 percent mark. The public's esteem for Congress during that year plunged to 8 percent, an all-time low.

In 1995, then, partisanship achieved new high levels, going into the 90s for the GOP in the House. The Republicans in the Senate flirted with the 90 percent range. The Democrats in both bodies were quite far from it, well into the low 80s. To be precise, Democrats in the House voted with fellow Democrats 80 percent of the times, whereas Democrats in the Senate voted with their fellow Democrats 81 percent of the times. Republicans in the House voted with their fellow Republicans 91 percent of the times, a watershed moment for party unity since this was the first time that a party had entered into the 90s range in these data. Republicans in the Senate voted with their fellow Republicans 89 percent of the times. In response, the public's confidence in Congress in 1995 barely made it into double digits, standing at 10 percent.

In the late 1990s and into the new century, both parties in both chambers continued to register their party unity averages well into the 80s and even approaching the mid-90s in some cases. In 2001, for instance, House Democrats averaged their party unity at 83 percent for the year, whereas the House Republicans stood at 91 percent. Senate Democrats stood at 89 percent and Senate Republicans were at 88 percent. The confidence level in that year registered at 18 percent. In 2003, House Democrats averaged at 87 percent, and House Republicans averaged once again at 91 percent. In the other chamber, Senate Democrats stood at 85 percent, but the Senate Republicans ended the year at 94 percent, an all-time high in recent memory. As for the confidence level in that year, it stood at a mere 20 percent.

In effect, party unity scores reaching into the 90s or even into the high 80s means that almost all Democrats vote with their party and almost all Republicans vote with their party almost all the time. Indeed, such has been the saga in recent years. Also, the consistency in rise in partisanship and the decline in confidence is once again revealed in Table 5.2. As Democrats and Republicans became more and more partisan, public's regard for the institution dropped. As an aside, note that in these data, the Republicans reached into the 90 percent in more than one year; the Democrats never did. Indeed, the Republicans peaked higher than the Democrats in these data. Party unity scores reached the 94 percent mark, the peak, for the Senate GOP in 2003, and topped off at 91 for the House GOP in several years. The Democrats, in either body, never entered the 90s range in these data. These figures suggest that the Republicans became partisan before the Democrats did, and they were more so than the Democrats.

In addition, Table 5.3 shows figures about the extent to which one party unanimously voted against a majority of the other party and its impact of confidence in Congress. The idea here is that unanimous partisan voting represents the increasing gap, and hence the bitterness, between the two parties, which contributes to lowered confidence in the institution. Table 5.3 contains the data for this variable, combining the House and Senate unanimous votes.

As can be seen, as the frequency of unanimous partisan votes has increased in Congress, as the Democrats and Republicans have more often united to oppose the other side, moving firmly into the triple digits since 1993, confidence in Congress has dipped to consistently low levels.

Undoubtedly the clearest signs of the consistently increasing divide between the two parties and the resulting decline in confidence in Congress are seen in the data presented in Table 5.4. The relationship between the two variables is once again clear and consistently inverse. Table 5.4 reveals the ideological positions of the two parties in the two chambers in the postwar years.[13] As can be seen, Democrats and Republicans in the House have grown more and more apart during these years, as have Democrats and Republicans in the Senate, resulting in less and less confidence in the institution.

In 1965–66, the ideological position of House Democrats stood at −0.24955 and the ideological position of House Republicans stood at 0.24920. For the Senate Democrats, it stood at −0.27107, and for the Senate Republicans, it stood at 0.24821. These are quite moderate scores, much closer to zero than the scores of today. The respect for Congress during that year stood at 42 percent. The divide between the parties from then on begins to consistently grow. The numbers for Democrats in both bodies become higher and higher on the negative side, and for the Republicans in both bodies, they become higher and higher on the positive side (with a temporary drop for the Senate GOP for a few years).

In 1983–84, the ideology of House Democrats grew more liberal, standing at −0.29940, and that of the House Republicans became more conservative, standing at 0.32846. Likewise, for the Senate Democrats,

Table 5.3
Unanimous Partisan Votes and Confidence in the Modern Congress

Year	Total Unanimous Votes	Confidence in Congress
1966	14	42
1967	20	–
1968	10	–
1969	15	–
1970	7	–
1971	20	19
1972	14	21
1973	85	–
1974	1	18
1975	46	13
1976	7	9
1977	15	17
1978	5	10
1979	22	18
1980	39	18
1981	60	16
1982	17	13
1983	36	20
1984	23	28
1985	45	16
1986	13	21
1987	68	20
1988	73	15
1989	26	16
1990	63	14
1991	63	9
1992	87	16
1993	164	12
1994	101	8
1995	343	10
1996	124	10
1997	147	11
1998	129	12
1999	233	12
2000	139	15
2001	159	18
2002	126	22
2003	365	20
2004	181	13
2005	301	16
2006	196	10

Note: Unanimous voting data taken from *Congressional Quarterly Weekly Report*, January 1, 2007, 38, and previous CQ Almanacs; confidence data taken from The Harris Poll, March 1, 2007.

Table 5.4
Ideological Extremism and Confidence in the Modern Congress

Year (Congress)	House Democrats	House Republicans	Senate Democrats	Senate Republicans	Confidence in Congress
1965–66 (89th)	−0.24955	0.24920	−0.27107	0.24821	–
1966					42
1967–68 (90th)	−0.23428	0.24048	−0.27038	0.18138	–
1968					–
1969–70 (91st)	−0.25470	0.24883	−0.25895	0.16127	–
1970					–
1971–72 (92nd)	−0.25622	0.24375	−0.25415	0.14883	19
1972					21
1973–74 (93rd)	−0.28017	0.24875	−0.29805	0.18836	–
1974					18
1975–76 (94th)	−0.28828	0.23850	−0.29520	0.19297	13
1976					9
1977–78 (95th)	−0.28086	0.23878	−0.28774	0.18497	17
1978					10
1979–80 (96th)	−0.28316	0.27048	−0.28938	0.20461	18
1980					18
1981–82 (97th)	−0.28973	0.29572	−0.27733	0.25342	16
1982					13
1983–84 (98th)	−0.29940	0.32846	−0.28457	0.26182	20
1984					28
1985–86 (99th)	−0.31418	0.34591	−0.30413	0.27776	16
1986					21
1987–88 (100th)	−0.31346	0.35569	−0.31591	0.28468	20
1988					15
1989–90 (101st)	−0.31665	0.36321	−0.32784	0.30698	16
1990					14
1991–92 (102nd)	−0.32109	0.38386	−0.34338	0.32291	9
1992					16
1993–94 (103rd)	−0.34003	0.42272	−0.36072	0.35145	12
1994					8
1995–96 (104th)	−0.37026	0.46314	−0.38186	0.38778	10
1996					10
1997–98 (105th)	−0.38132	0.47741	−0.40878	0.43011	11
1998					12
1999–2000 (106th)	−0.37802	0.48485	−0.40538	0.42361	12
2000					15

Note: Ideological extremism data taken from Norman J. Ornstein, Thomas E. Mann, and Michael J. Malbin, *Vital Statistics on Congress 2001–2002* (Washington, D.C.: The American Enterprise Institute Press, 2002), 181–82; confidence data taken from The Harris Poll, March 1, 2007.

it stood at –0.28457, whereas for the Senate Republicans, it stood at 0.26182. The data for confidence in Congress during those years dropped to 20 percent in 1983 and 28 percent in 1984, as the ideology of the two parties rose. The confidence in Congress in the 20s would still be considered quite respectable by today's standards.

The ideological extremism of the two parties continued to grow, reaching into the "3" range for the first time for both sides in 1989–90. The House Democrats reached the ideological position of –0.31665, and the House GOP stood at 0.36321. Similarly, the Senate Democrats reached the ideological mark of –0.32784, and the Senate GOP stood at 0.30698. In turn, the public's respect for Congress in 1989 was at 16 percent, and dropped to a relatively low number of 14 percent in 1990. Indeed, after 1989–90, the ideological numbers never go below the "3" range for either political party in either chamber, and the confidence number usually hovers in the low teens.

In 1993–94, the ideological position of the House GOP reaches into the "4" range, but remains in the "3" range for the House Democrats and for both parties in the Senate. The House Democrats stood at –0.34003, whereas the House Republicans stood at 0.42272. The Democrats in the Senate were at –0.36072 and the Republicans in the Senate were at 0.35145. The public's esteem for Congress in 1993 stood at 12 percent and dipped to an all-time low of 8 percent in 1994. After 1994, the public's esteem for the institution remains low.

For the final years in the data in Table 5.4, 1999–2000, the ideological extremism score is into the "4" range for all but one group, the House Democrats. They stood at –0.37802, whereas the House Republicans stood at 0.48485. The Senate Democrats stood at –0.40538, whereas the Senate Republicans stood at 0.42361. The public's confidence in the institution stood at 12 percent in 1999 and mildly higher, at 15 percent, in 2000.

The data in Table 5.4 show a consistent rise in extremism on both sides, producing a consistent decline in confidence in Congress. That has been the fundamental hypothesis of this chapter and this book, and it has been handsomely confirmed. As an aside, it is also important to note that the ideology grows more extreme for the GOP first, i.e., the numbers rise for the GOP before they do for the Democrats. The Republicans entered the "3" range before the Democrats did, and again they entered the "4" range before the Democrats did. Furthermore, the ideological extremism is greater on the GOP side than it is on the Democratic side. In 1999–2000, the House Republicans very nearly approached the 0.5 mark, standing at 0.48485, representing the most extreme conservatism. The Senate Republicans stood at 0.42361. The House Democrats never even entered the "4" range in these data, topping off at −0.38132 in 1997–98. The Senate Democrats barely entered the "4" range, topping off at −0.40878 in 1997–98. As shown in Table 5.2 with reference to party unity scores, these data also show that the GOP took the lead in extremism, and the Democrats followed suit. These are small but noteworthy points.

The fundamental hypothesis forwarded herein, that increased partisan polarization in Congress produces lowered confidence in and respect for the institution, is confirmed by other studies as well. In a study based upon three laboratory experiments, Diana Mutz and Byron Reeves examined the effects of televised political disagreements on levels of political trust. Mutz and Reeves conclude: "Political disagreement is inevitable and unavoidable, and also quite desirable from the perspective of most democratic theory. In this study we examined the hypothesis that it is the *manner* in which such disagreement is presented that discourages positive attitudes toward politics and politicians. The results of these experiments show that uncivil political discourse has detrimental effects on political trust" (emphasis in original).[14] Moreover, in an effort to gain prescriptive recommendations from this study, if incivility reduces trust, can civility increase trust? As Mutz and Reeves note, "[i]ndeed, if one envisions the cumulative impact of repeated exposure to incivility, then low levels of political trust are not surprising. On the other hand, to the extent that civil political discourse is equally prevalent, one would expect these effects to cancel themselves out."[15]

Based upon his examination of survey data, David King also finds a conclusive link between partisanship and political trust. King wrote in a beautifully conducted analysis, "Trust in government is related to partisanship in two ways."[16] First, strong partisans show higher trust than weak partisans. That has always been the case, as strong partisans display higher levels of emotional attachment to their party than weak partisans do. Second, King tested the ideological distance between all people in a National Election Study survey and "the closest group of strong partisans" in that survey. "The prediction is that the smaller the distance, the greater the trust. As the parties have polarized, more and more Americans have seen the parties drift away from their centrist preferences." His findings attested that the "results...are unambiguous on this point. The more distant the parties are from respondents, the more likely respondents are to say that they mistrust government, even after accounting for the effects of unemployment, education, age, year, partisan strength, and so on."[17]

King further extends the hypothesis that polarization produces mistrust by examining data on split-ticket voting. "The results there also indicate that the further away one is from both parties, the more likely a voter is to vote for candidates from more than one party. Political scientists are nowhere near a consensus on the causes of split-ticket voting....In exploring the causes of mistrust, however, both mistrust and declining fidelity to parties appear driven by thirty years of polarization."[18]

More directly on the point of polarized debate and declining respect for Congress, Gary Orren lays the blame squarely on public officials, who themselves ceaselessly demean each other and the very institutions in which they serve. Unprofessional political discourse, therefore, diminishes the politicians and the institutions. Orren argues, "Politicians attack one another with even more venom than they unleash at the government. Harsh and uncivil discourse has become a staple of campaigns and governing, sending out negative messages that polarize the electorate while turning off substantial portions of the population. In the process, politicians erase their own credibility. 'After all,' the public reasons, 'it takes one to know one.'"[19]

John Hibbing and Elizabeth Theiss-Morse provide an extensive examination of the public's attitudes toward Congress and other American political institutions. Their study is based upon their own detailed nationwide survey and focus group data. When asked how Congress was doing handling the most important problems facing the country, 75 percent of respondents (3 out of every 4) gave Congress a "poor" grade, and only 2 percent gave it a "good" grade.[20] In the same survey, when questioned about members of Congress, 61 percent of the respondents (3 out of every 5) said they were "disgusted" with Congress, and nearly the same amount (60 percent) said they were "angry" at Congress. Only 14 percent said they were "proud" of members of Congress.[21] Moreover, only 30 percent of the respondents agreed while 57 percent disagreed with the statement that "Congress does a good job representing the diverse interests of Americans, whether black or white, rich or poor," and a whopping 78 percent agreed and only 15 percent disagreed with the statement that "Congress it too far removed from ordinary people."[22]

Such unflattering sentiments of both Congress and the members, according to Hibbing and Theiss-Morse, are partly a result of the conflict and bickering that take place in Congress. They conclude that people do not like the "process" by which Congress goes about doing its business. "People's views of the political system and of particular bodies within that system are shaped not just by policy outcomes, by the image of certain individuals, or by partisan loyalties, but primarily by the processes employed in the system and in the institutions."[23]

In his testimony on Capitol Hill on this issue, Hibbing remarked more broadly on the problems with conflict in politics and how the public views that conflict. According to Hibbing,

> [t]he point is that the political conflict and friction that people detest is not simply that found in a sometimes acrimonious Congress. Congress can improve its debating and decision-making processes, no doubt about that. But it is important to recognize there is a deeper problem here. People are not very comfortable with any type of conflict. They do not like it, whether it is Congress doing it or they are doing it themselves in a group of only about 60–70 people gathered together in a New England town meeting. Many people either do not like conflict or they do not think conflict is necessary.[24]

The link between partisanship and approval is, of course, not new. Roger Davidson, a Congress expert, has examined both old and new data about this relationship. In an older study of the fluctuations in public regard for Congress from the 1940s to the 1960s, Roger Davidson, David Kovenock, and Michael O'Leary note: "public approval is usually highest when domestic political controversy is muted....When partisan controversy is especially acrimonious, or when Congress seems slow in resolving legislation, public disaffection increases."[25]

In a newer study, with data from the 1990s, Davidson again laments the problem of partisanship and its corrosive effects on Congress. In the 1990s, of course, Congress was much more partisan than it was in the 1940s or the 1960s. Speaking of the newcomers, Davidson writes: "Once they arrive on Capitol Hill, newly elected members become immersed in an intensely partisan community. Congress is organized and led by its political parties."[26] All the perks and powers in Congress are doled out on a partisan basis. Moreover, "[b]ecause demographic shifts have altered their electoral bases, the parties have grown more distinct in their positions, and more militant in their policies and ideologies."[27] According to Davidson, "[t]hese partisan and ideological chasms result not only in sharp divisions in floor votes but also in harsher language and 'take no prisoners' political tactics."[28] The result, a more divided Congress and more public disapprobation of the institution.

Looking at trends on the declining public approval of Congress, Kenneth Mayer and David Canon also investigate the lack of popularity of the institution. And partisan bickering is one of their explanations as well. "Why is Congress so unpopular?" they want to know. The answer they provide rests on many factors, including partisan squabbles. "Many contemporary accounts argue that it is because Congress is fundamentally corrupt and inefficient, and that legislators as a group are dishonest, incompetent, quarrelsome, and more interested in self-aggrandizement than solving problems. A more charitable explanation is that members want to do the right thing but are handcuffed in their efforts by archaic procedures, an entrenched and ossified congressional elite, and partisan wrangling."[29]

Robert Samuelson, a columnist for the *Washington Post,* provides a superb analysis of the effects of polarization. The result, according to him, "is a growing disconnect between politics...and ordinary life." In a polarized setting, "[p]olitics is increasingly a world unto itself, inhabited by people convinced of their own moral superiority," on both the left and the right of the political scale. In such an atmosphere, "[t]heir agendas are hard to enact because they're minority agendas. So politicians instinctively focus on delivering psychic benefits. Each side strives to make its political 'base' feel good about itself." To Samuelson, consequentially, "[p]olarization and nastiness are not side effects. They are the game. You feel good about yourself because the other side is so fanatical, misguided, corrupt and dishonest."[30] This game plays out every day, and the public loses patience and respect.

Finally, Bill Bradley, former senator from New Jersey, also draws the connection between heightened partisanship and the drop in confidence in and respect for the government. As a former practitioner of politics, Senator Bradley is well aware of the problems of partisanship. He writes, "[o]ur political process is at a standstill. Democrats and Republicans both march along the well-worn paths of symbolic politics, waving flags labeled 'welfare,' 'crime,' and 'taxes' to divide Americans and win elections. Underlying the paralysis of government is a collapse of trust. Democracy is paralyzed not just because politicians are needlessly partisan. The process is broken at a deeper level, and it won't be fixed by replacing one set of elected officials with another."[31]

———•———

The data presented in this chapter convincingly reveal that senseless partisan quarrels have resulted in lowered public esteem of Congress and its members. As partisan division on both sides of the aisle has grown, public regard for the institution and its members has dropped. The two are intimately connected. Of course, the public's confidence in Congress compared to other institutions of American society has been considerably low to begin with (see Table 5.5) and public esteem of being a congressman or a senator compared to other occupations is also quite low to boot (see Table 5.6).

So what does lowered confidence in and respect for Congress mean?

The United States Congress is the symbol of American democracy, and diminished public confidence and respect for this institution undermines the very system of American government. The Congress of the United States is to be held in high regard, not reviled at every opportunity. As the nation's premiere lawmaking body, lowered public esteem threatens to only further sideline the leading institution

Table 5.5
Public Confidence in Institutions

	% Having "A Great Deal" or "Quite a Lot" of Confidence
The military	68
Organized religion	58
The police	57
The U.S. Supreme Court	49
The presidency	49
Banks	43
The medical system	40
Public schools	36
Television news	34
Newspapers	33
Big business	30
Organized labor	28
The criminal justice system	23
Congress	26

Note: The Gallup Poll, June 10, 2000.

Table 5.6
Public Esteem of Occupations

	% Indicating "Very High" or "High" Levels of Ethics and Honesty
Pharmacists	69
Medical doctors	58
College teachers	52
Auto mechanics	24
Local office holders	20
TV reporters	20
Labor union leaders	17
State office holders	16
Lawyers	13
Car salespersons	8
Congressmen	11
Senators	17

Note: The Gallup Poll, November 4–7, 1999.

of American government. Lowered respect for Congress and its members means less regard for what they do. Diminished esteem for what they do means less respect for the very system of government. All these factors can contribute to reduced legitimacy of the institution. That should be a cause for concern to everyone.

The argument is not at all that one should simply revere Congress at every occasion and not criticize it. Healthy criticism is always good. Mindless finger-pointing is not.

CHAPTER 6

THE IMPACT OF PARTISAN WARFARE ON THE LEGISLATIVE PROCESS

And these few precepts in thy memory
See thou character. Give thy thoughts no tongue,
Nor any unproportion'd thought his act.
Be thou familiar, but by no means vulgar.

Give every man thy ear, but few thy voice;
Take each man's censure, but reserve thy judgment.

This above all: to thine own self be true,
And it must follow, as the night the day,
Thou canst not then be false to any man.
William Shakespeare, *Hamlet*, act 1, sc. 3, 58–61,
68–69, 78–80

The essence of lawmaking in Congress is deliberation.
Thomas Mann and Norman Ornstein,
The Broken Branch

Upon his retirement from the U.S. Senate, Howell Heflin, former Democratic senator from Alabama, noted the following:

> The bipartisanship that is so crucial to the operation of Congress, especially the Senate, has been abandoned for quick fixes, sound bites, and, most harmfully, the frequent demonization of those with whom we disagree.... The focus on divisive issues has increased the alienation and driven us farther and farther apart. In my judgment, much of the answer to this alienation lies in what I call "compassionate moderation." Instead of being so concerned with policies that are "left" and "right," government should be concerned with the principles of right and wrong, which come from

approaching issues in measured, moderate, and compassionate tones. . . .
Our Constitution itself came about through a series of great compromises;
it was not written by ideologues who clung to "their way or no way."
Compromise and negotiation—the hallmarks of moderation—aimed at
achieving moderate, centrist policies for our country, should not be viewed
as negatives. They should be valued, for that is the only way to reach
consensus on complicated issues and problems that face us.[1]

The previous chapter illustrated the first of two major consequences
of increased polarization noted in this book. That chapter showed
how partisan divisiveness has lowered public esteem of the nation's
first branch of government. This chapter is about the second key
consequence of increased polarization: the deleterious effect on the
legislative process.

In this chapter, my express aim is to discuss how good legislating is
done, should be done. What are the qualities needed for a successful
legislative process? Conversely, what makes for bad legislating? Why
is the absence of ingredients necessary for good legislating a problem?
It is clearly evident that the qualities needed for a productive legislative
process are increasingly missing. Lack of civility and trust reign
supreme, making negotiating and deal-making all but impossible. The
public suffers, as problems remain unresolved. A successful legislative
process is all about trust and compromise, and there is the rub.

———◆———

Former Congressman Lee Hamilton, a member of the old school,
makes an articulate, albeit not a novel, case for compromise.
He writes:

At its best, politics is not a matter of holding on to your opinions no matter
what; it's the art of finding common ground with people who think differently, then forging a workable approach to resolving a problem. . . . In a nation
as big and diverse as ours, in which people hold so many differing opinions,
that means finding solutions to issues that allow us to work peaceably and
productively together; and that means finding compromises. . . . [Members]
usually discover that it is difficult to be effective in Congress unless they
learn how to build consensus. . . . Members who don't learn the art of compromise usually find themselves on the margins of the legislative process. . . .
Legislating is not like war, in which one side strives to impose its will on
the other. It is a shared path, the route we all must follow as we try to live
with one another and struggle together to resolve the difficult questions that

confront us. Good politicians look for solutions that allow both sides to claim, if not victory, at least some gains. They seek accommodations among rival interests, because they know that it's necessary to make the country work. And they recognize that creating permanent enemies would make it difficult, if not impossible, to enlist help on future issues from those they opposed in the past....A willingness to compromise is nothing more nor less than the recognition that we're all in this together for the long haul, and that each of us has a stake in the system by which we govern ourselves.[2]

In another instance, Hamilton wrote:

You might ask, if Congress is simply reflecting the society around it, why should we worry that it has so much trouble making civility its norm? *Because on Capitol Hill, the ability to work together directly affects both the quality and the quantity of the work that gets done. Incivility and outright rudeness make it virtually impossible to reconcile opposing views and, therefore, to achieve legislative goals or produce good legislation. In an atmosphere rife with distrust and unpleasantness, it becomes all the more difficult to discuss complex issues, search for reasonable solutions or build the consensus needed to pass them.* (emphasis added)[3]

Across the aisle, former Senator Robert Dole, the Republican leader from Kansas, also spoke of the need for compromise in the legislative process. On the occasion of his departure from the Senate following a thirty-five-year distinguished congressional career, Dole remarked:

I think sometimes around here we think we have to have everything. "We have to have total victory. I will not settle for less. It has to be my way, or no way." Well, Ronald Reagan said once, "If I can get 90 percent of what I want, I would call that a pretty good deal." Ninety percent is not bad. You can get the other 10 percent later. It is a small amendment then. Better understand that—take the 90 and then work on the 10.[4]

No one knew better when it came to getting the deal done than Senator Dole.

––––•••––––

So what are the necessary ingredients of a successful legislative process? One might surmise a few essential qualities. Clearly, experience, expertise, seniority, leadership position, and perhaps some other objective variables would stand out as necessary. Experience helps to know the ins and outs of the legislative process. Going around the tracks a few times puts one above those who have not. Expertise helps too, for knowing the ins and outs of an issue gives one the potential to persuade colleagues to win more votes. Seniority and leadership positions bring power of their own. Many political scientists have properly documented the significance of these variables in the legislative process.

To this list, however, it is undoubtedly vital to add the more subjective characteristics such as friendship, trust, goodwill, and the ability and willingness to negotiate and compromise. It is highly likely that these may be considered to be more important than the various formal variables identified above. These characteristics represent the grease that grinds the often slow, laborious, and cumbersome legislative process.

Indeed, political scientists Gregory A. Caldeira and Samuel C. Patterson theorize as follows:

> Because legislative institutions must process a multitude of complex and controversial issues in an orderly and civil fashion, their effective performance rests upon strong networks of friends. *Interpersonal ties among members define the legislature,* laying the basis for the dynamics of legislative leadership, supplying the texture for partisan and other aggregations of members, establishing channels of communication, and providing the connections through which bargaining, exchanges of cues, and decision making transpire. (emphasis added)[5]

Accordingly, effective functioning of everything that a legislature does is based upon these informal elements of friendship and trust and compromise and so on.

Another political scientist, Ross K. Baker, also underlines the value of friendship and camaraderie in the legislative process. He hypothesizes as follows. According to Baker, much of what happens in an effective legislative process is the result of what he calls "institutional kinship." He defines that as relations that

> arise out of professional pride, collegiality, and a satisfying business relationship....Institutional kinship is a friendship based upon the *esprit de corps* that comes from having been elected to a prestigious institution and the accommodations that are so valuable in achieving success there.... Institutional kinship, then, in the broadest sense is the expression of pride at being part of a select institution—a pride which is accentuated by the ordeals of initiation common to all. But it is quite clearly more than simple esprit de corps; it is a relationship whose origins are found in the interdependence of senators.

Baker adds, "[i]nstitutional kinships are relationships based on trust and dependability."[6]

So what are the advantages of this kinship? Baker answers, "[t]he political value of forging with a colleague an alliance spanning both party and ideology is particularly great in the legislative world.... Based upon a track record of trust derived from shared experiences, these peculiar friendships enable senators to save time in gathering information and cues and reduce transaction costs in their dealings with colleagues. Life in the Senate is simply easier in the company of a few trusted colleagues."[7] And how does this happen?

> The cloakrooms, dining rooms, and various recreational facilities and watering-holes provide settings in which relationships of a strictly business nature can be softened and humanized. They also allow the exposure of a less public side of members, enabling senators who know their colleagues only as the embodiments of certain regional or ideological viewpoints to deal with them in an environment in which these characteristics are less ostentatiously on display. Senators can let down their hair, establish personal rapport, and even lay groundwork for compromise and cooperation, all of which may not be possible in the more sunlit arenas of the floor and committee rooms.[8]

Baker continues:

> What can realistically be asked of senators by way of friendship with their colleagues is trust, integrity, hard work, and a decent tolerance for those with whom one differs. This is what friendship means, instinctively, to most senators.... This form of friendship, which has been referred to here as institutional kinship, is more than simply a good business relationship or a "political friendship." It is a more complicated form of human association, which for many senators comes to define the meaning of their experiences in the Senate. Rather than pointing to a single legislative accomplishment, a particularly hard-fought and dearly won battle, or an interest staunchly defended, senators often look back on their careers and evaluate them in terms of this kind of friendship.[9]

Baker illustrates his hypothesis based upon a great deal of evidence derived from biographies, historical accounts, and personal interviews, all strongly supporting the notion that interpersonal ties among members are the bread and butter of making the legislative process work.[10]

Not only political scientists, practitioners also most certainly value the importance of trust and goodwill in the legislative process. One Republican lobbyist with close ties to the Senate noted, "if you don't have trust, you're not going to be able to get anything done in this town."[11] Speaking specifically about the Senate, another veteran observer remarked, "[n]othing gets done without comity, compromise, mutual regard and a willingness to listen."[12]

These are, therefore, the virtues that guide an effective legislative process. Trust and compromise are vital. The willingness to talk and to listen, to negotiate and to bargain, or to put it more rawly, to cut deals, that is the crux of the matter!

A good example of how the legislative process worked, and indeed can work, came in 2005. During the spring of that year, the Senate was facing a showdown over the use of filibuster in connection to judicial nominations. A number of senators were attempting to avert this showdown but faced a difficult struggle not due to lack of experience or skill but due to lack of goodwill and mutual regard. In reporting this incident, Dan Balz of the *Washington Post* emphasized the significance of trust during the talks. "In an era of polarized politics, in which party and congressional leaders have been increasingly responsive to their most ideologically driven activists, the bipartisan band of senators has attempted to steer a different course. Behind closed doors, they have tested whether it is possible to find language to codify the principles of trust and goodwill at a time when little of either is left in the political system."[13] Lacking trust, Balz continued, "[t]he argument is not insignificant. Democrats believe that asking Republicans to rule out the nuclear option while preserving their own right to filibuster is justified because the filibuster is part of Senate rules and that option means changing the rules. Republicans believe that makes the deal unbalanced in the Democrats' favor. The negotiators have tweaked and tinkered with words, but trust, rather than language, is at the heart of the impasse."[14]

Referring to the same set of negotiations, Charles Babington of the *Washington Post* wrote, "[n]egotiators said the toughest task is building sufficient mutual trust among the dozen so they feel confident that neither side will renege on or abuse an understanding that cannot be written in air-tight legalisms."[15] In the same report, Babington cited Norman Ornstein, saying that the deal between the two sides was tricky "because it requires a leap of faith on the part of senators, because there are no guarantees here."[16]

In the same case, David Brooks of the *New York Times* also empha-
sizes the spirit of compromise and deal-making as necessary to a
successful legislative process. As a long-time observer of politics,
he writes:

> There are two ways the Senate can work. The Senate could be a legal
> battleground in which the two parties waged all-out struggles to rig the
> procedures so they got what they want....Or the Senate could be the home
> of informal arrangements. In this model, leaders of the two parties would
> get together—yes, often in secret—and make reasonable bargains. They
> would rarely settle things on pure principle, but they'd hope for agreements
> in which each side achieved a portion of its goals.[17]

He observes, "[t]his backroom deal-making model went out of fashion
after Watergate, but it is much better than what's come since."[18]
    In this celebrated case, the senators brokered a deal. They did so
because, at the end of the day, at least a handful of them were able to
brush aside their partisan differences, trust each other, and think of
the institution. According to a veteran observer:

> The unusual pact between the rank-and-file senators, headed by McCain
> and Nelson [Democrat Ben Nelson of Nebraska], was the result of a series
> of causal encounters and unusual, shifting alliances. Drafts were written,
> picked apart, rewritten and picked apart again. Escape clauses for Republi-
> cans and Democrats were drafted and sometimes tossed aside. Names
> of judicial nominees to be let through were floated in every possible
> combination. Details were added and then scaled back to keep the deal from
> sinking under its own weight...."This happened because there was a
> group of us that thought the institution, and the very fundamentals of the
> institution, were at stake," said McCain.[19]

Lindsey Graham of South Carolina said, "To me, it was just silly where
we got ourselves. You know, we got into the third-grade playground
politics, and I think we're now at the fifth grade. And maybe we'll
get to high school one day."[20] The deal proclaims: "Such a return to
the early practices of our government may well serve to reduce the
rancor that unfortunately accompanies the advice and consent process
in the Senate."[21]
    When the ingredients of trust and compromise are not present,
there are tremendous negative consequences for the legislative
process. Things do not get done, major issues facing the country

remain unresolved, the public suffers, and partisan bickering persists. The rise in party unity, as illustrated in the previous chapter and discussed throughout this book, has significantly contributed to the lack of deal-making, and therefore effective legislating, in Congress.

David Broder argues that extremely high partisanship, and hence the lack of trust and willingness to compromise, "raises doubt about the government's ability to address any of the major challenges facing the country." The issues are many, and far-reaching:

> The layoffs...at Ford, coming after those...at General Motors and Delphi, spell out the threat to America's industrial base. Runaway health care costs for the automakers' retirees are a big part of the problem, but a Congress racked by partisanship has been stuck in neutral on systemic health reform....The same thing is true when it comes to Social Security, energy policy and management of the federal budget. Party-line votes in all these areas have become the basic pattern....In the House, the subjects that provoked disagreements included immigration rules, stem cell research, surveillance and interrogation policies, arms sales to China, the Central American Free Trade Agreement (CAFTA), the Endangered Species Act, energy, and the intervention in the Terri Schiavo case. In the Senate, the parties split on class-action lawsuits, bankruptcy protection, CAFTA, the USA Patriot Act, the budget, defense appropriations, energy, and the nomination of John Bolton to the United Nations.[22]

The list is long and distinguished.

Others agree. Robin Toner, writing for the *New York Times*, states that the lack of bipartisan coalitions has made it virtually impossible to solve the major problems facing the nation. "Older senators talk wistfully of a more civil era that they say has now largely vanished. The few remaining centrists say the fierce partisan currents make it very hard to build the bipartisan coalitions necessary to do something big—like changing Social Security—or to defuse internal disputes like the present one over judges."[23] James A. Thurber, a political scientist, blames the leadership. To him, then Senator Frist "ha[d] not shown himself particularly adept at bridging the gap between moderates and conservatives or mending fractures in the GOP's own coalition. That is one big reason for the lock-up over energy, the overhaul of tort law and other issues....I think the institution will continue to be in crisis—a crisis of civility and comity. There will be no incentive to reach toward the center and compromise."[24]

Indeed, compromise and deal-making are all too missing in the contemporary Congress, and that significantly hurts the legislative process. Both sides are afraid of making compromises, and each side blames the other for the absence of it. Both sides play the game of politics almost strictly from a partisan angle, with a sharp eye toward the ever-present next election. According to a veteran observer, "[o]n the GOP side, any move to compromise with Democrats is met by countervailing pressures to dig in and settle instead for confrontational votes that get the Senate nowhere but allow Republicans to dramatize their charges of Democratic 'obstructionism'—and make their case for voters to give Republicans a wider majority."[25]

In an atmosphere that is devoid of trust and the willingness to cut deals and get things done, the temptation for both sides, be it Democrats or Republicans, whoever has the majority, is to stifle debate as much as possible. Instead of talking to each other, as would be necessary to accomplish things, the urge, however incomprehensible it sounds, is to not talk. And perhaps even more importantly, the majority usually desires to prevent the other side, the minority, from talking. Moreover, the majority does what it wants, especially in the House, and the minority has no choice but to accept. The attempts to control and limit debate, ironic for a legislative body and the legislative process, are increasingly the order of the day in both chambers.

Table 6.1 contains data showing the rise in restrictive rules in the U.S. House over the past thirty years. The growth in restrictive rules, and the decline in open rules, is clearly an attempt by the majority to limit input, in the form of debate or amendments, on legislation, especially from the minority. As can be seen in Table 6.1, during the 95th Congress, in 1977 and 1978, the number of open rules was 179, constituting 85 percent of all rules granted in the House. That number and percentage has witnessed a sharp decline since then. In the 109th Congress, in 2005 and 2006, the number of open rules was merely 22, a small fraction of the number granted just over a quarter century ago, constituting only 16 percent of all rules approved. On the other hand, the number of restrictive rules in the 95th Congress stood at 32, making up only 15 percent of all rules granted. By the time the 109th Congress rolled around, a dramatic shift had occurred. The number of restrictive rules jumped to 116, nearly four times the number in the 95th Congress, making up a whopping 84 percent of all rules granted.

The persistence of increase in restrictive rules, and the concurrent drop in open rules, prompted Democrats on the House Rules Committee, the panel in-charge of granting these rules, to issue a report in

Table 6.1
The Growth of Restrictive Rules in the House

Congress and Year	Open Rules Number	Open Rules Percent	Restrictive Rules Number	Restrictive Rules Percent
95th, 1977–78	179	85	32	15
96th, 1979–80	161	75	53	25
97th, 1981–82	90	75	30	25
98th, 1983–84	105	68	50	32
99th, 1985–86	65	57	50	43
100th, 1987–88	66	54	57	46
101st, 1989–90	47	45	57	55
102nd, 1991–92	37	34	72	66
103rd, 1993–94	31	30	73	70
104th, 1995–96	86	57	65	43
105th, 1997–98	72	51	70	49
106th, 1999–2000	93	51	91	49
107th, 2001–2002	71	37	71	63
108th, 2003–2004	33	26	95	74
109th, 2005–2006	22	16	116	84

Note: Data taken from Roger H. Davidson and Walter J. Oleszek, *Congress and Its Members,* 11th ed. (Washington, D.C.: Congressional Quarterly, 2008), 252.

March 2005 where they labeled Republicans as "the more arrogant, unethical and corrupt majority in modern congressional history.... What sets the 108th Congress apart [when only 22 percent of all rules granted were open rules, the lowest since the Republicans took over the House in 1994] from its predecessors is that stifling deliberation and quashing dissent in the House of Representatives became the standard operating procedure."[26]

Even some GOP members dislike the increasing use of restrictive rules. Congressman Gil Gutknecht, Republican from Minnesota, chided his own leadership, saying: "Here we are fighting for democracy in Iraq and Afghanistan and we have more and more closed rules here. We don't want democracy to flourish on the floor of the House of Representatives."[27]

A similar picture emerges in the U.S. Senate. Table 6.2 contains data showing cloture votes. A call to invoke cloture is an attempt by the majority to limit debate on a nomination or a pending piece of legislation. These data are for much of the postwar era. In the 82nd Congress, in 1951 and 1952, there are no calls for cloture. By the time the 92nd Congress rolled around, there were twenty attempted clotures, but only four were successful (having reached the minimum votes needed to invoke cloture). Throughout the 1980s and the 1990s,

Table 6.2
The Growth of Cloture Votes in the Senate

Congress and Year	Attempted Clotures	Successful Clotures
82nd, 1951–52	0	0
83rd, 1953–54	1	0
84th, 1955–56	0	0
85th, 1957–58	0	0
86th, 1959–60	1	0
87th, 1961–62	4	1
88th, 1963–64	3	1
89th, 1965–66	7	1
90th, 1967–68	6	1
91st, 1969–70	6	0
92nd, 1971–72	20	4
93rd, 1973–74	31	9
94th, 1975–76	27	17
95th, 1977–78	13	3
96th, 1979–80	21	10
97th, 1981–82	27	9
98th, 1983–84	19	11
99th, 1985–86	23	10
100th, 1987–88	44	12
101st, 1989–90	24	11
102nd, 1991–92	49	23
103rd, 1993–94	42	14
104th, 1995–96	50	9
105th, 1997–98	51	18
106th, 1999–2000	57	27

Note: Data taken from Norman J. Ornstein, Thomas E. Mann, and Michael J. Malbin, *Vital Statistics on Congress 2001–2002* (Washington, D.C.: The American Enterprise Institute Press, 2002), 152.

the attempts to invoke cloture as well as success at achieving cloture continued to rise. During the 106th Congress, in 1999 and 2000, there were fifty-seven formal attempts to cut off debate, and twenty-seven of them were successful.

The clotures are invoked to cut off filibusters, or the privilege of extended debate, in the Senate. The employment of filibusters is a time-honored tradition, giving the minority, and even individual senators, a voice and a right to unlimited debate in the Senate. It is a precious right enjoyed by the minority. The growing invocation, and approval, of clotures suggests a trend toward limiting the voice of the minority. This, of course, inflames those on the short end of the stick, be they Democrats or Republicans. In theory, however, even conservatives recognize the importance of filibusters to the minority, and indeed to the democratic process. As conservative columnist George F. Will has argued, "[t]he filibuster is...an instrument for minority assertion. It enables democracy to be more than government-by-adding-machine, more than a mere counter of numbers. The filibuster registers intensity, enabling intense minorities to slow or stop government."[28]

In practice, though, both sides continue to attempt to use clotures and stop filibusters when they are in-charge and it serves their agenda, with major adverse effects for the legislative process. These tactics are no doubt intended to frustrate and delay the legislative process, and each side blames the other for the delay. When Trent Lott was the Republican majority leader, the Democrats fired with verbal rounds at him. "Democrats complain that Lott has distorted the Senate's natural rhythms by immediately filing cloture motions that would limit debate and amendment opportunities."[29] When Bill Frist followed Lott as the GOP's leader, he too became part of the blame game. "The day of the failed cloture votes, Frist took Democrats to task for tactics he called obstructionist. He and other Republicans say they are willing to allow votes on Democratic proposals—just not a limitless list....Democrats, for their part, say they are only asking for a fair and open process and charge that Republicans are trying to stifle debate. They say Republicans are just trying to avoid tough votes on overtime and other issues."[30]

In addition to these two obvious trends (the increasing use of restrictive rules in the House and clotures in the Senate) to stifle debate in Congress, the majority party, particularly the Republicans in both bodies in recent years, have strenuously fought to exclude Democrats from the conference committees. The conference committees are ad hoc committees created around major pieces of bills to resolve legislative differences between the chambers. They are supposed to include members of both parties, from the committees of jurisdiction, from both the House and the Senate. However, fearing dissent and delay, the Republicans would rather not include the Democrats in that vital step in the legislative process. "Observers in both parties, including former lawmakers and staff, say more intense partisanship in both chambers has undermined comity and collegiality that in the past fostered cooperation in conferences. More issues today are being resolved at the leadership level or are being 'pre-conferenced' by the party in power, with the full conference just a formality." "I think it's probably not good," said a former aide to the Senate Republican leadership, who became a lobbyist in Washington.[31]

Former Senator Breaux, who had been included in conferences by the Republicans due to his moderate positions on issues, also laments this trend. And to the extent that moderates from either party are included, they seem to be just token inclusions. "More and more conferences are majority-party driven. That's not the purpose of conferences. They're meant to be a give and take. I've been included, but it's all Republicans in the room," said Breaux. He added, "there is at best a gloss of bipartisanship."[32] In this case, on a plan in 2003 to add a prescription drug care benefit to Medicare, in addition to Breaux, Senator Max Baucus, a Democrat of Montana, was included largely because they both supported portions of the legislation. However, Daschle, then Senate minority leader, and Senator John D. Rockefeller IV, a West Virginia Democrat, both members of the Senate Finance Committee, were denied participation in the conference. Also excluded was Charlie Rangel, the New York Democrat and the ranking minority member on the House Ways and Means Committee. Responded Rangel, "What they're saying is that they will just ram it down our throats."[33] The exclusion of the other party is very harmful to the process. Traditionally, the minority party has had a choice in sending its conferees; the majority party is not supposed to dictate the minority party's membership on conference committees. Even some Republicans argue that the minority party's views ought to be considered as legislation is crafted and voted upon. Says former Congressman Leach, the Iowa Republican, "I personally believe that process is our most important product, and when one doesn't pay a lot of heed to process, problems of governance escalate."[34]

Finally, aside from exclusion from conference panels, the Republicans have altogether attempted, led by their leadership, to squash any efforts to listen to dissenting views or consider language from the minority on the standing committees. The excluded members are mostly Democrats, but also those in the GOP with whom the leadership disagrees. In one case, in early 2005, Congressman Brian Baird, Democrat of Washington, offered a constitutional amendment addressing the question of replacing members if large numbers died or were incapacitated by a terrorist attack. The House Judiciary Committee is the committee of jurisdiction in this matter. However, its chair, Republican James Sensenbrenner Jr., of Wisconsin, opposed the amendment. He offered his own version instead, on the same issue. Moreover, to carry matters further, he used his power as committee chair and declined Baird an opportunity to speak on his alternative before the committee. Baird responded, "Common courtesy would say if you're discussing someone's bill you ought to let him speak on it. It is cowardice and bullying to do otherwise."[35] Baird's proposal, however, being in the minority, lost overwhelmingly in the committee, while Sensenbrenner's measure passed the House by a margin of 329 to 68 votes.

When Barney Frank, the Massachusetts Democrat, proposed an amendment in the House Financial Services Committee in 2005 calling on Fannie Mae and Freddie Mac "to devote 5 percent of their after-tax profits to creating affordable housing," the amendment passed the committee by a handsome margin of 53 to 17. Even many Republicans on the panel joined the Democrats in support of the amendment. However, some conservative Republicans opposed it and went to the leadership, seeking to discard the amendment in the Rules committee. They succeeded, and the bill passed over Frank's objections.[36]

The Republicans have devoured their own as well. In 2003, Iowa's Leach, the former chair of the House Financial Services Committee, proposed an amendment to a banking bill "to strengthen federal over-sight of lending institutions known as 'industrial loan companies.'" The Rules Committee turned him down. Leach said the committee's decision was scandalous. He noted, "I consider it an embarrassment to the House that this issue cannot be debated on the most important banking bill that is going to be debated before this Congress this year." When in 2005, Jeff Flake, a conservative Republican of Arizona, pro-posed a measure "allowing U.S. citizens the right to send personal-hygiene products to relatives in Cuba," the House GOP leadership took it upon itself to deliberately distort his proposal. It was considered to be a popular amendment, and the leadership feared its passage. When the measure came up for a vote, senior Republicans circulated a flier on the House floor "suggesting the measure would allow 'unfettered trade with the communist regime of Cuba with no Administration oversight of said trade.'" To which Flake furiously responded, "I don't mind losing a fair fight. When your own party puts out that kind of garbage it's really troublesome....There's a lot of underlying frustration beginning to bubble up among lawmakers."[37]

Indeed, even some governors, Republicans and Democrats alike, are now expressing contempt for Congress. Governors tend to be par-ticularly sensitive to legislative process because they have to get things done. They actually have to solve matters. At a meeting of the National Governors Association in 2006, Republican governors had nothing but disdain for their Republican brethren who then controlled Congress.

Then-Governor Mike Huckabee of Arkansas commented, "What upsets us is the same thing that frustrates our voters. Whatever problem you're concerned about, all you see in Washington is gridlock." Former Governor Mitt Romney of Massachusetts likened the two parties in Congress to "two guys in a canoe that is headed for the falls, and all they do is hit each other with their paddles. The bickering is becoming more and more dangerous because the current is sweeping us toward the falls." Democrats pounded their scorn likewise. Governor Janet Napolitano of Arizona said: "They're just not getting it done. Immigration is the biggest issue in my state. A million people are marching in the streets. States are spending hundreds of millions trying to cope with the influx. So they pass two bills, and they won't even go into a meeting room to put them together. It's ridiculous!" Governor Bill Richardson of New Mexico observed, "Congress has gone from unresponsive to hopeless. On everything from the minimum wage to immigration to energy, they've just given up. No one expects anything from them."[38]

No one expects anything from Congress because Congress appears to be preoccupied with playing politics rather than making policy. It is easier to strategize to demean your opponents than to sit down with your opponents to discuss constructive solutions to major public problems. Legislating is bitter and partisan and it almost appears to be an afterthought in how the House and Senate do business these days.

Former Senator Breaux nostalgically recalled how business was done during the days when his fellow Louisianan, Senator Russell B. Long, chaired the Senate Finance Committee from 1966 to 1981: "They broke out the bourbon and walked out with a deal." But that is not how today's conservative Republicans see it. Said then-Senator Santorum of Pennsylvania, a staunch Republican: "This idea that somehow or other, irrespective of who's in the majority, that this is an egalitarian place, that everybody has a seat at the table all the time, it's just not the way this place operates. The majority means something. It means that you win."[39]

Such arrogance by the majority only produces defective legislation. The point of the matter is that legislating cannot be done in a distrustful, vindictive, partisan environment. At least not good legislating anyway! Good legislating is a long and tedious process that requires endless hours of give-and-take, countless debates and negotiations, and, in the heart, a desire to solve problems. In the gut, it requires faith in the other side and the willingness to take what you can get today and leave the rest for tomorrow.

The trends identified above (of restrictive rules, clotures, exclusion from conferences, exclusion of anyone who disagrees with the leadership) are extremely disturbing for a legislative assembly.[40] As Norman Ornstein has said, "It's not just that it offends me that they're shutting people out. It's that you end up with bad legislation."[41]

Toward the end of *The Broken Branch*, Mann and Ornstein state:

> The decline in deliberation has resulted in shoddy and questionable policy—domestic and international. The unnecessarily partisan behavior of the House majority has poisoned the well enough to make any action to restrain the growth of entitlement programs and to restructure health care policy impossible and has badly strained the long tradition of bipartisanship on foreign policy....The failure of both houses of Congress to do meaningful oversight contributed to the massive and unconscionable failures of the Department of Homeland Security and, after Hurricane Katrina, of its FEMA arm.[42]

They conclude with the following: "The broken branch distresses us as long-time students of American democracy who believe Congress is the linchpin of our constitutional system."[43]

So how is good legislating done and who are the good legislators? Legislating, as Lee Hamilton says, is an art. Legislative success requires legislators to listen to others, particularly those with whom they disagree, to trust each other, to find compromises. In April 2006, *Time* magazine produced a remarkable study identifying "America's 10 Best Senators." The magazine based its study on a variety of factors, chiefly the ones noted above.

The ten best senators recognized by *Time* include such well-known senators as Arizona Republican John McCain, Pennsylvania Republican Arlen Specter, Indiana Republican Richard Lugar, Illinois Democrat Richard Durbin, Maine Republican Olympia Snowe, among others. One stands out for being the mainstreamer, another for being the contrarian, another for being the wise man, and so on. One, however, in particular stands out for being the deal-maker.

No one would have thought that Massachusetts Democrat Ted Kennedy would be identified as "the deal-maker." Kennedy is nationally known for his liberalism. He has, perhaps mistakenly, the persona of a hard-edged Democrat, who always fights with the Republicans and is never successful at anything he does. Insiders, however, know that Kennedy is an extremely accomplished legislator, who has worked with many in the GOP in his long congressional career on significant pieces of legislation. He has done so because, despite his very partisan persuasion, he has been willing to cut deals at the end of the day. According to *Time*, "the key to his legacy is not that he is determined to stick up for his principles. It's that he is willing to compromise on them." As *Time* tells it, Kennedy

> has amassed a titanic record of legislation affecting the lives of virtually every man, woman and child in the country. With a succession of Republicans, he helped create COBRA, the Americans with Disabilities Act, portable health care, the Family and Medical Leave Act and more than 15 key education programs....He also pushed through the deregulation of the airline and trucking industries and the reduction of the voting age to 18. By the late '90s, the liberal icon had become such a prodigious cross-aisle dealer that Republican leaders began pressuring party colleagues not to sponsor bills with him.[44]

Another observer notes:

> In the public consciousness, Kennedy's persona may be that of the unflinching liberal warrior, champion of government-based solutions and red-faced berator of Republican nominees. And he is, when that's called for (and, at times, when it's not). But this Kennedy caricature is misleading because it is incomplete. Into his fifth decade in the Senate, he is a dogged, pragmatic practitioner of the legislative arts. Kennedy-McCain on immigration, Kennedy-Romney on health care (the Massachusetts senator worked behind the scenes to get the necessary federal go-ahead and also as an emissary to hostile state Democrats leery of giving Romney a big win)— these aren't aberrations but simply the most recent examples of Kennedy cross-party collaboration....Kennedy is "a throwback," says one longtime Democratic strategist who uses the term admiringly (and who has never worked for the senator). "He grew up in an era when you tried to get things done. Now we try *not* to get things done, on the theory that somewhere down the line, if we take over, we'll be able to get things done." (emphasis in original)[45]

Kennedy, hence, relies on deals and compromises in the legislative process.

The same *Time* study praises other senators it lists as the ten best for their spirit of compromise and bipartisanship. For example, among

Senator Durbin's good qualities are that he "has a bipartisan side." He has worked with Senator Santorum, former conservative Republican from Pennsylvania, "to push the U.S. government to give $500 million in additional funds for the Global Fund to Fight AIDS, Tuberculosis and Malaria." Early in 2006, "he helped broker a compromise between Democrats and Republicans to reauthorize the USA Patriot Act, working on a provision that will keep most libraries from having to hand over information about users without an order from a judge."[46] In another case, "[b]ecause of her centrist views and eagerness to get beyond partisan point scoring," Senator Snowe "is in the center of every policy debate in Washington." Her "formula of being clued into the center and into home have made her very popular in Maine."[47]

As a matter of fact, legislative success in the Senate comes precisely due to all these qualities. Deal-making and compromise are as necessary as air and water. As one longtime observer has noted, "[i]t has never been easy getting legislation through this most august of governmental bodies, and so the smart senator always knew that collegiality and cooperation had to transcend ideology or partisan impulse. You never knew when you might need the help of another senator, however divergent his view of the world might be from yours."[48]

In that vein, members who want to achieve legislative success model their legislative careers with those qualities in mind. Take, for instance, the case of Senator Hillary Clinton, the New York Democrat. Having arrived on Capitol Hill after being the First Lady of the United States for eight years, she had every right to a celebrity status. Moreover, given her standing in the Democratic Party, she could have taken the position of partisan warrior and fight for the liberal causes. However, she understood that success in Congress comes by way of compromise, not by way of confrontation. Veteran observers say that her record "is more nuanced than her many opponents describe. While she is among the most dependable of Democratic votes, she has defied at times the expectations of both the right and the left. She has been an increasingly outspoken critic of the Bush administration, but she has also shown herself to be a nuts-and-bolts policymaker, willing to compromise, work behind the scenes and strike pragmatic alliances with even her husband's staunchest foes to move her agenda."[49]

Indeed, as difficult and as personal as it might be, Senator Clinton has found ways to work with some of the staunchest conservatives in the House and Senate, many of whom were fiercely critical of her husband's presidency. She has worked with Senator Lindsey Graham on health care issues for the families of the members of National Guard and Reserve; with Senator Sam Brownback, a conservative Republican from Kansas, on human rights matters; with Senator Robert Bennett, a Utah Republican, on an anti-flag burning legislation; and with Senator John Sununu, a Republican from New Hampshire, on child safety issues. Also, she teamed up with Senator Santorum on examining the effect of media on children, with former Republican Senator Don Nickles on federal unemployment benefits, with former House Majority Leader Tom DeLay on foster care system, and with former Republican Speaker of the House Newt Gingrich and former Senate Majority Leader Bill Frist on electronic medical records.[50] All of that because she understands that trust and comity are the only ways to get things done in Congress.

In fact, Senator Lindsey Graham, who as a member of the House led the impeachment against President Bill Clinton, and Hillary Clinton have formed a bond on a number of legislative matters, especially those dealing with troops and veterans. Said Senator Graham: "The past is the past. She's been very gracious. And I would say that if you're willing to work with her, she seems to be very receptive to working with you."[51]

For a counterpoint, take the case of Bill Thomas, former Republican congressman from California. On his retirement, David Broder wrote: "Thomas is an able, principled conservative who has pushed through major legislation that has changed the direction of national policy and altered millions of people's life prospects. He is also someone who has inflicted substantial damage to the legislative process and to personal relationships on Capitol Hill, leaving bruised feelings in his wake." During his career, Thomas had his fingerprints on many major pieces of legislation, ranging from tax cuts to trade authority to prescription drug benefit in Medicare.

> All of those measures were and are controversial, but no one can dispute that Thomas's imprint on the legislation—and, therefore, on American life—has been significant. The achievement, though, has come at a price. What was once a committee [the mighty House Ways and Means Committee which Thomas chaired] whose institutional pride was far greater than its partisan divisions has become a bitter political cockpit, where major national policy is set by party-line votes, rather than through patient negotiation and discussion.[52]

"Personally prickly and often impatient, Thomas quarreled bitterly with colleagues of both parties, but especially with some of the senior Democrats on his committee." Largely due to that, the Democrats refused to compromise with Thomas on Social Security reform efforts in 2005. "No bridges had been built between the parties, no basis established for bipartisan talks on an issue of genuine national importance." Broder ends his story on this powerful legislator with a sad statement: "Now, facing a Republican-imposed term limit on his tenure as chairman, Thomas is quitting at 64, at the height of his vast intellectual and political powers. You have to wonder how much more he could have accomplished without the strong-arm tactics and how much less damage he might have caused."[53]

Yes, indeed, you have to wonder!

CHAPTER 7

DEMOCRACY
IS A CONVERSATION

He that of greatest works is finisher
Oft does them by the weakest minister:
So holy writ in babes hath judgment shown,
When judges have been babes; great floods have flown
From simple sources, and great seas have dried
When miracles have by the greatest been denied.
Oft expectation fails and most oft there
Where most it promises, and oft it hits
Where hope is coldest and despair most fits.

William Shakespeare, *All's Well That Ends Well,*
act 2, sc. 1, 139–47

A vibrant democracy is a messy spectacle, dependent on grease,
horse manure, and prestidigitation.

Joe Klein, *Politics Lost*

In *Fight Club Politics,* Eilperin highlights the current problems within
the institution of Congress, noted throughout this book, in the following fashion:

> Republicans and Democrats did get along better before Jim Wright became
> Speaker....And Gingrich and his deputies did transform the Hill's social
> network by urging junior members to keep their families at home....
> But House Democrats also helped poison the well over the past decade, by
> pursuing ethics claims against Gingrich and feuding over the appointment
> of the House chaplain in 1999. These scuffles...sowed distrust between the
> two parties....In addition, broad institutional changes...have eroded the
> bonds that used to foster comity on Capitol Hill....Thirty years ago, new
> members were more likely to move their families to D.C. after an election.
> They were eager to become part of the capital's social scene and wanted
> their spouses and children near to where they spent most of their week.

Families often socialized with each other regardless of party, and these personal ties curbed members' tendency to demonize each other. If Wisconsin Democrat David Obey attacked Representative Willis Gradison (R-Ohio) on the House floor, his wife Jane would lambaste him at home, pointing out that they were likely to have dinner with the Gradisons later in the week. This sort of lifestyle disappeared in the late 1980s and early 1990s when GOP firebrands like Dick Armey declared themselves members of the "Tuesday to Thursday Club" and spent as little time as possible in Washington. They chose to sleep in their offices rather than waste money on a proper apartment, and they sharply questioned why their colleagues would relocate to the nation's capital....At the same time members started rushing to catch their Thursday flights back home, they began shunning congressional trips abroad that have traditionally provided another avenue for bipartisan bonding....Members not only stopped sharing free time together over the past decade, they found themselves debating each other less often on the House floor....A typical House floor debate now is more Kabuki theater than genuine discussion....In this new climate, politicians have an easier time characterizing one another as devious, ignorant, or dangerous.... Washington politics has reached the point at which name-calling offers tremendous rewards and minimal cost, encouraging lawmakers on both sides to engage in it.[1]

It is pretty clear from the preceding chapters that Congress has indeed been behaving badly over the last few decades. Members of Congress have done about as much as they can do to demean the institution, ridicule their colleagues, and obstruct the legislative process. Not all members are obviously guilty of this, but many are.

In the foregoing chapters, I have described the increasingly partisan and uncivilized debate in the corridors of Congress, with members using harsh personal attacks to question each other's motives. I have also shown how, in the past few decades, Congress has been occupied less and less by old style members who appreciated the value of negotiation and compromise and become home more and more to new style members who are eager to confront for the sake of ideological purity at the cost of getting things done. After identifying many causes underlying the rampant partisanship and vitriolic behavior, I have discussed at length the two fundamental consequences of partisanship and incivility, one being the decline in institutional respect by the public and the other being the deleterious effects on the legislative process.

My purpose in this final chapter is to offer some solutions designed to curb partisan warfare and to make a plea for pragmatism. I start this chapter by showing how democracy is meant to be based upon conversation and end with showing how pragmatism is the only way to make a democratic society function most effectively. The middle is about the reforms.

It seems to be exceptionally fitting to title this chapter "Democracy is a Conversation." Democracy is, indeed, a conversation. It is not based upon fiats, it is not based upon dictates, it is not based upon fatwas. A democratic system of government assumes, and as a matter of fact respects, or should respect, the idea that people have different values, principles, and beliefs. In an open society, there is nothing that can be done to prevent the free and uninhibited airing of these values, principles, and beliefs. That is in fact what democracy is all about. The differences in ideas and perspectives are to be accepted, they are to be cherished, they are good. They make a democracy better. They make for better solutions to public problems, they make for a better functioning of representative institutions of government. They do require, however, that people deal with those differences in a civil and mature fashion, if everyone's differences are to have a place in the marketplace of ideas.

The best way to deal with people, who in a democratic polity will undoubtedly come to the table with different perspectives and thoughts, is not to quash the opinions of some but rather to accept them. But if everyone's viewpoints and judgments are to be accepted, are considered worthy in debate, how then can solutions to public problems be arrived at the end of the day that necessarily must contain only one policy, must necessarily provide only one course of action? For after all, there cannot be 2 different, or 100 different, or 435 different courses of action. The basic answers, the most elementary, the most commonsense answers lie in such factors as compromising, negotiating, and bargaining. In a democratic society, to get anything done, it is incumbent upon everyone to be willing to compromise.

In recent years, compromise in some quarters, particularly among the believers in ideological purity, is thought to be a bad thing. It is viewed, or it is sold, in negative, pejorative terms. It is assumed that if one compromises in the political arena, one is selling out on his or her political convictions. That one somehow takes his or her political beliefs lightly. That one is ready to toss his or her principles out the window simply for the sake of political expediency. Such charges are patently inappropriate and unfair. It is absolutely essential to have principles, but one cannot completely refuse to budge on those principles unless a person lived alone on an island. The fact of the matter is that to live, to conduct business, and to thrive in any society which consists of two or more people would require all of them to compromise. Otherwise, nothing would get done. The truth of the matter is simply that no two people think alike. No marriage, no relationship in the world would ever work if both people were unwilling to ever give in even a bit on anything. The same principle applies to legislation and to governing. Good relationships work, good legislation gets passed only if both sides are willing to converse to work out their differences in an amicable fashion.

There is nothing at all wrong with compromise. It is not a bad thing; it is not a dirty word. I would argue that compromise is not about giving in, it is not about losing. Compromise is about gaining something. If no one compromised, no one would get anything. Compromise, therefore, is about achieving something that one would not otherwise have. As the saying goes, half a loaf is better than none.

The necessity of bargain and compromise, based upon the precept of free exchange of ideas in a democratic society, is all the more important in a complex country such as the United States. In a society with people from many different backgrounds, many different cultures, many different walks of life, nothing would ever get done if everyone held steadfastly to their guns. Indeed, even the most casual scan of the history of the United States would show that any major, productive, consequential decision taken in this country is a product of give and take. The Constitution of the United States, just to take one example, that remarkable document produced in the summer of 1787 in Philadelphia, is certainly a product of a series of compromises. After all, federalism was nothing but a compromise, the Great Compromise was clearly a compromise, the Bill of Rights is also the result of a compromise. The Founding Fathers vigorously debated these issues, they had genuine disagreements about the different courses of action, but in the end they worked out their differences by talking and by giving in a little to get something.

To say that democracy is a conversation is, of course, neither new nor revolutionary. There is nothing groundbreaking here. The idea of democracy as a conversation has been loudly and skillfully articulated by many observers over the course of human history. It has been the subject of countless books, conversations, and theories. In practice, nevertheless, especially in modern American politics, in contemporary debates in the committees and on the floors of the House and Senate of the U.S. Congress, the idea is frequently forgotten.

The requirement of democracy as a conversation is reflected in many scholarly debates on the topic. It has a long tradition, to be sure, and it continues to this day. The Fall 2004 issue of the *Hedgehog Review* was devoted to this subject. The editors writing the introduction to this special issue, entitled "Discourse and Democracy," observed that "in a democracy, we agree not to kill each other over our differences. We choose, rather, to engage each other in open, public, substantive discussion and debate. The operating assumption is that we can work out disagreements through persuasion rather than coercion. Public discussion, debate, and argument, then, are at the heart of America's great political experiment in self-rule." The editors further noted an obvious, but presently all-too-forgotten corollary: "It is not just that we talk—how we talk is every bit as important. The reason is that language both reflects and shapes social reality, framing how we think about experience. The means by which the dialectic of public discourse takes place, then, shapes the nature and formation of political reality. Thus, democracies are deeply affected by the kinds of public discourse that occur within them."[2]

In the same issue, Christopher Nichols offers a cumulative definition of deliberative democracy, based upon the viewpoints of such varied political theorists as Hannah Arendt, Jon Elster, Jurgen Habermas, and others. Writes Nichols,

> [w]hile definitions vary, deliberative democracy is, in short, a system of political decisions premised on collective contemplation of a series of alternatives. The idea is to straddle the line between, on the one hand, a pragmatic understanding of the process of consensus decision-making and, on the other hand, the simple plurality of opinions or votes expressed across the large representative democracies of the 21st century. Participants in the deliberative process are obliged to offer arguments persuasive to others and respond to counter-arguments. They are not obliged to come to consensus, only to modify their beliefs in light of their deliberative interchanges.[3]

Many others echo similar views. In the words of James L. Connor, S.J., director of the Woodstock Theological Center, "[c]ivil discourse...is a precondition of a democratic society."[4] In early 1776, John Adams, one of the nation's most revered Founding Fathers, wrote to a friend about a fundamental danger in a democratic polity. He said,

We may please ourselves with the prospect of free and popular governments, God grant us the way. But I fear that in every assembly members will
obtain an influence by noise rather than sense, by meanness rather than
greatness, and by ignorance and not learning, by contracted hearts and not
large souls. There is one thing, my dear sir, that must be attempted and most
sacredly observed, or we are all undone. There must be decency and respect
and veneration introduced for persons of every rank, or we are undone.
In a popular government, this is our only way.[5]

In the same report, Thomas Mann writes,

Democracy is a means of living together despite our differences. Democratic
deliberation is an alternative to physical violence. It's predicated on
the assumption that it's possible to disagree agreeably,...that one can
vigorously contest the positions of one's adversary without questioning
his or her personal integrity or motivation, and that parties to a debate are
entitled to the presumption that their views are legitimate if not correct....
Vigorous debate is supposed to be followed by good faith efforts at negotiation and bargaining.

He asks, "But does that mean civil discourse must necessarily be
boring, centrist, non-partisan, reverential of authority? Certainly
not," he says. In developing this argument, Mann adds, "I would
argue just the opposite. It's incivility that frustrates the democratic
ambition of fully airing honest differences. It's difficult to focus public
attention on choices among legitimate alternatives when rhetoric
is dominated by personal demonization. Civility is no obstacle to
passionate advocacy, partisanship, wit, and yes, even humor, but it
requires some agreement on fundamentals, and it certainly requires
mutual respect."[6]
    "Democracy is about improving government through the uninhib-
ited exchange of ideas," writes E.J. Dionne of the *Washington Post*.[7] As
Norman Ornstein has stated, "[t]he Framers designed a deliberative
democracy, with deliberation having multiple meanings—policymaking through vigorous give-and-take debate and policymaking
done slowly with all deliberate speed." Ornstein explains exactly
how that is supposed to work. "The idea of the Framers was not to
have government decisions reflect public opinion, but to produce a
public judgment, reached after extensive discussion, disagreement
and debate that would enlarge upon and refine public views." A good
decision, a good law, takes time and effort. "The slow and deliberate

process of debate and give-and-take, done face to face by representatives from different areas and disparate constituencies, allows all
perspectives and interests to be weighed. The process of persuasion
and building laborious coalitions, the Framers thought, would result
in decisions more just and more likely to stand the tests of time and
legitimacy with citizens."[8]

In contemporary political culture, however, some see an almost
complete absence of deliberation. Todd Gitlin argues that

> [d]eliberation is scarce in the halls of government and in the surrounding
> public realm. A joint press conference by the chief presidential candidates is
> considered a "debate." Orations by members of Congress to empty Senate
> and House chambers are considered "debate." The mere jousting of opinions
> is considered "debate." Professional interlocutors—news anchors and jour-
> nalists—do not consider it seemly to press political protagonists to confront
> the reasoned objections of their opponents. Politicians repeat canned phrases
> whatever the questions. Harangues substitute for intellectual encounters.

He continues, "[f]or a politician, the premium is on circulating the
themes and auras—not arguments—that arouse followers and remind
the political base that he is their guy. The point of political speech
today is not to persuade, not to refute counter-speech—not even to
address it—but to arouse an emotional response. Sloganeering is—or
is believed to be—the most reliable means to galvanize the base. The
intent is not Socratic but Pavlovian."[9]

Such is indeed the state of conversation in modern American
politics. There is little democratic deliberation in the House and Senate.
Neither side wants to converse with the other; each would rather
simply impose its will on the other. The factors discussed widely
throughout this book, and specifically in chapter 4, contribute to this
dilemma. It is a dilemma because there is a real need to talk to each
other, not past each other. House districts are drawn in such a way that
there is no need for Democrats to cater to Republicans, and vice versa.
The media love shouting and conflict, not negotiating and compromise. Conflict grabs people, compromise is boring. The political
consultants encourage confrontation, so do the interest groups.
Everyone is busy campaigning, feverishly running for the next
election, using hot-button social issues to divide for personal gain
rather than to unite for national gain. There is no socializing among
members; there are precious few real friendships that cross party lines.
If members talk to those on the other side, it is to question their

motives. There is no conversation, no trust, and without conversation and trust, there can be no resolution of complex public problems. Indeed, the premium these days in the legislative process is on each side to exclude those from across the aisle rather than to include them. As David Brooks has argued, "[i]f you drive people out, you *will* have a polarized situation in Washington. You can learn something by bringing in people who are not within your zone....There is...virtue in having conversation." (emphasis in original)[10]

What must be done to stop incivility in American politics? What must be done to limit the extremely harmful effects of crude partisanship and blame-game in contemporary politics on Capitol Hill? Let me suggest the following measures as the ideas for reform designed to deal with the culprits of cannibalism, the six factors identified in chapter 4 as the causes of Congress behaving badly.

The road to reform is never easy. It is always an extremely bumpy one. Noted political scientist Morris Fiorina argues that "[p]olitical scientists are notoriously loath to suggest reforms. As a profession we tend to be conservative with a small 'c.'"[11] If that be the case, let me be a radical and depart from my political science friends and boldly, albeit perhaps foolishly, suggest some badly needed reform measures.

Without a doubt, a major step toward fixing the problems of incivility and partisanship would be to fix the nation's redistricting process. That would be a first giant step toward greater electoral competition, toward increasing cross-party cooperation, and toward more public trust in the institution of Congress. As Mann and Ornstein write, "[c]ompetitive districts and states tend to produce more moderate elected officials, ones less driven by ideological agendas and more inclined to listen to voters and groups on both sides of the partisan divide. Increasing the level of electoral competition is a worthy objective for those who want to mend the broken branch."[12]

Redrawing the district lines in a nonpartisan or a nonideological fashion would indeed make a difference in the nation's politics. According to Mann and Ornstein,

> [l]awmakers have become more insular and more attentive to their ideological bases as their districts have become more partisan and homogeneous. Districts have become more like echo chambers, reinforcing members' ideological predispositions with fewer dissenting voices back home or fewer disparate groups of constituents to consider in representation.

> The impact shows in their behavior; and reform of the way in which
> legislative boundaries are redrawn would make a difference.[13]

Says Eilperin, "[c]reating more seats with competitive general-election
contests would give aspiring politicians an incentive to move a little
closer to the political center, which in turn could at least foster a more
meaningful dialogue on Capitol Hill. That change could reduce the
echo-chamber effect that now exists between House members and
their like-minded constituents."[14]

There appears to be a unanimous agreement among all impartial
observers that the way House districts are redrawn in this country is
broke and is in dire need of repair. The question is, who should do it
and how should it be done?

Most observers believe, and the record shows, that it is unlikely that
Congress or the Supreme Court will take charge of this matter. Notes
Eilperin, "[m]any advocates are calling for a national redistricting
system, complete with uniform standards that limit redistricting to
once a decade and place a priority on fostering competitiveness,
maintaining communities of interest, creating geographically compact
districts, and reflecting the state's true political balance. Only two
institutions could impose such national standards: the Supreme Court
and Congress."[15] The Supreme Court, in its decisions in *Davis v.
Bademer* (1986) and in *Vieth v. Jubelirer* (2004), either has set very high
standards to judge partisan gerrymandering or has been unable to
agree when a district is gerrymandered in a partisan fashion. To Mann,
"the federal courts do not appear a promising venue for reform.... In
past decisions, the Court has explicitly sanctioned the protection of
incumbency as a legitimate redistricting objective."[16] Congress, for
its part, is not likely to do so, certainly not at the risk of losing House
seats for incumbents.

But if the Congress and the courts will not step into this fray to
mandate some level of nonpartisan or nonideological drawing of lines
by state legislatures and governors, who would do it then? To most
neutral voices, the answer is an independent commission. As Mann
has written before at length,

> [a] healthy degree of party unity among Democrats and Republicans has
> deteriorated into bitter partisan warfare. With the number of moderates in
> legislative bodies declining, the possibilities of bipartisan negotiation and
> compromise diminish. Many observers and participants believe redistrict-
> ing fuels this polarization, by creating safe seats in which incumbents

have strong incentives to reflect the views of their party's most extreme supporters—i.e., those active in primary elections—and little reason to reach out to swing voters.

Mann argues that "clearly most promising avenue of reform is to change the process by which states draw legislative maps. Often facing entrenched opposition in state legislatures, reformers are increasingly turning to the initiative process to establish independent, nonpartisan redistricting commissions."[17]

Mann appears to prefer the approach employed in Arizona for redistricting reform. In Arizona, an independent commission is created to apportion the district lines. The commission is made up of four appointed members (two from each party, chosen by the state legislature from a list approved by a judicial committee), who then select a fifth person as chair. The chair comes from a different but comparable pool of candidates and is not affiliated with either political party. The commission works by majority vote, and neither the legislature nor the governor have a say in how those maps are drawn.[18]

Eilperin, too, refers to the Arizona model, in addition to the ones from Iowa and New Jersey, although she does not seem to express a preference for one or the other. In Iowa, the staff of the nonpartisan Legislative Service Bureau draws the map every ten years after the census, without taking any political data (party registration or incumbents' domiciles) into account. The state legislature then can approve or reject the plan, but cannot amend it. If the legislature does not approve it, the Legislative Service Bureau can redraw it. Again, the state legislature can only approve or reject it. If rejected, the bureau can come up with a third map. The legislature has the right to modify the third attempt. However, the state legislators in Iowa have rarely changed a proposed plan. The state Supreme Court gets involved only if the process does not work or if the proposed plan is patently unfair. New Jersey offers a simpler alternative. The state creates commissions to draw maps, with equal number of members from both political parties. The state Supreme Court appoints a tiebreaker, traditionally a political scientist from Princeton University or Rutgers University. If the tiebreaker has no agenda, the commission produces a map fair to all sides. In the end, Eilperin seems to lean toward an independent commission rather than leaving the redistricting process at the mercy of Congress or the Supreme Court.[19]

Fiorina, too, takes the independent commission route. Indeed, he would eliminate the role of the state legislatures altogether (and for that matter, of governors also) in the redistricting process. To him, a major "avenue toward moderating American politics would be to remove redistricting from the purview of legislatures and place it in the hands of (preferably nonpartisan) appointed commissions. But rather than have the legislature approve the final plan, skip the legislature and submit it to popular referendum."[20]

William Brock, a former congressman and senator from Tennessee and chairman of the Republican National Committee from 1977 to 1981, also prefers an independent commission. In a *Washington Post* article, he said:

> The absence of any contest has contributed to the increasing absence of voters: Why bother? The impact on civility and civil discourse, on constructive debate and comity, is even more pernicious. The pattern of redistricting as it has evolved leads to such results....If a candidate need talk only to those who are most fervent in support of the party, he or she doesn't have to listen to, or even speak to, people in the center, much less those of the other party. As a matter of fact, candidates seen cozying up to people on the other side of the political aisle might put their own primary prospects at risk.

Brock concludes that because of the current redistricting system, "the result is less dialogue, less comity and more partisanship. Anyone who doubts this has not been paying attention to the 'debates' in Congress over the past decade or so."[21] He puts his faith in the Iowa model.

Even some lawmakers see virtue in having districts that are more mixed than similar. Brian Baird, the Washington Democrat, has said: "It makes your life worse, but it makes you a better person. We are a country of loggers and environmentalists, Christian fundamentalists and liberal agnostics, union activists and anti-union business people. Living in a district where you have to listen to people of diverse perspectives is more indicative of the country as a whole." Mixing the districts is very likely to make members more bipartisan than partisan, with members naturally inclined to reach consensus and be civil. John Tanner, a centrist House Democrat from Tennessee, noted: "I don't give my voting card to Nancy Pelosi, and I don't expect Republicans to give their voting cards to Denny Hastert [the former speaker]. This is not a Democratic or Republican political convention here. This is where the people's business is being done."[22]

Fixing the process of how congressional districts are drawn will be a major first step in rebuilding the political center, thereby engendering political compromises across the aisle and reducing the mean-spiritedness in Congress. My view in that regard would be to push for an independent commission, perhaps of the New Jersey kind, to do the job. (As a political scientist, I like the idea of having a political scientist as a "kingmaker" in the process!) But, in fairness, that would permit both parties to have a voice in the process but not control it, while at the same time reflect the preferences of the state's inhabitants.

The next area of challenge is the role of political consultants during the electioneering and the governing processes. Political consultants are increasingly employed by candidates and public officials to provide advice, to do polling, to engage in fund-raising, and to generally consult the politicians on a host of other political activities. The advice and services they provide are no doubt valuable, and politicians no doubt need it. Many political consultants are no doubt very skilled at their trade. The problem with consultants, in my judgment, is not their talent but rather their role in the political process on questions of accountability and democracy. Consultants tend to peddle what is good for the short-run, play on the public's momentary emotions, and will do almost anything to produce a victory for their clients.

From my perspective, the onus in this regard ought to fall on the candidates and public officials rather than on political consultants. It is the candidates and the public officials who have the higher burden with regard to the democratic and accountability aspects for this country, not the consultants. While I cannot go so far as to call for a ban on political consultants, as others have, I would suggest that politicians ought to employ consultants only sparingly and recognize the harmful effects that consultants bring about on the political process. It is up to the politicians to think about the long-term for this country. Their focus must not be on producing momentary victories for themselves or for their parties.

Regarding interest groups, *Congressional Quarterly Weekly Report* published a cover story with the title, "A Government Out of Touch." The subtitle to this story read, in part, "Washington is increasingly disengaged from the public, thanks in large part to interest groups' power." As John Cochran, the author of this report, wrote, "[g]roups aligned with the Republican Party include anti-abortion activists, evangelical Christians and the National Rifle Association; those close to Democrats include abortion rights groups, environmentalists and labor unions. In both parties they exert an influence beyond their

numbers—sometimes grooming and financing candidates early in
their careers....As the cost of campaigning has grown, so has the
influence of activist groups that can marshal contributions."[23]

On the particularly explosive issues, such as abortion, gay marriage,
stem cell research, and so on, the political right tends to push hard,
especially on judicial nominations. "The interest groups the party is
aligned with will countenance no accommodation on judicial nominations," writes John Cochran in another story. In 2005, the right leaned
heavily on then GOP Senate majority leader Frist to get their favorite
nominees through the U.S. Senate. Richard Lessner, executive director
of the American Conservative Union, said, "[i]f he aspires to the nomination [at the time, Frist was interested in seeking the Republican
presidential nomination in 2008], it's a test he has to pass [get the
nominees through]. This is pass-fail. He doesn't get a grade here.
He can't get a C for effort. He needs to deliver on this."[24]

Consequently, the basic truth of the matter is that, in contemporary
politics, the interest groups' grip on politicians seems to be exceptionally tight. The current circumstance, therefore, is exactly the opposite
of why interest groups were created in the first place. As discussed
in chapter 4, interest groups came about because the have-nots in the
society appeared not to have a seat at the table. Hence, interest groups
were seen as representations of pure democracy. They were seen as
vehicles to provide representation to the underrepresented.

Today, however, interest groups are anything but that. By any sense
of the measure, interest groups now represent very narrow, particular
agendas, not the public at large. They represent the most active, the
most committed, the most organized segments of the society, not the
disorganized and the not-so-privileged elements. Indeed, for their
activities, interest groups rely heavily on human and monetary contributions, which can mostly come from the most active and organized.
As Fiorina writes, "the political order that now exists in the United
States creates unnecessary conflicts and indulges itself in conflicts
that are the concern of relatively small numbers of unrepresentative
people. Often this comes at the expense of attention to conflicts that
concern larger numbers of citizens and leads to inattention to policy
solutions that would be widely viewed as progressive."[25] In addition
to the divisive politics that today's interest groups employ, their grip
on politicians is even more troublesome. In recent years, politicians
have relied on interest groups not only for electioneering activities
(campaign dollars, ads, manpower, and so on) but also for governing
activities (drafting legislation and so on).

In light of the interest groups' current activities, let me suggest the following reform ideas. Congress must, first and foremost, immediately pass legislation that deals with complete and full disclosure of all the perks and contributions that members receive from interest groups. Once the links between interest groups and public officials are fully disclosed, it matters less how much or what public officials receive from which interest group. As long as those links are fully exposed and are openly known to the public, the natural sunlight of the political process will automatically reduce the pernicious relationship between the two. Second, Congress must impose severe limits on a member's ability to introduce legislation. Specifically, members in the House ought to have at least fifty cosponsors from the other party and senators ought to have at least fifteen cosponsors from the other party before they are able to offer bills. This will bring a truly bipartisan flavor to the legislative process and reduce the excessive influence of the narrow and divisive interest groups.

Next, the news media, the talk-radio hosts, the bloggers, etc., in particular threaten the civil order of things. The news media thrive on conflict, on friction, on putting on a fight. That is what grabs viewers and boosts profits, but contributes nothing to pragmatic governance.

Norman Ornstein in particular is rightly worried that cyberdemocracy, the conduct of political debate on the Web, a popular aspect of the modern media, poses a great "challenge to deliberation.... Deliberation and cyberdemocracy are not easily compatible."[26] While Ornstein sees many pluses in the new medium, he also sees many minuses. "The Internet Age is like The Force in Star Wars. It has remarkable potential for good, enhancing the links between citizens and their representatives, enhancing the responsiveness of the legislative institutions, enhancing the information available to all about policy decisions." But, "there is a Dark Side, represented by a combustible combination of cynical distrust of institutions, populistic glorification of 'pure' democracy and the accelerating advance of information technology."[27]

As a prescriptive statement, Fiorina remarks that "[t]he media potentially could be of some use. When an activist spokesperson makes a pronouncement, a critical media could ask 'How many citizens do you speak for?' 'When did they appoint you as their spokesperson?' 'Have they approved your message?'" To him,

> [t]he media could even cease its unconsidered use of the neutral term "activist" and use terms that are often more accurate—exhibitionist,

crackpot, blowhard. None of this will come to pass however, for despite pious pronouncements about the role of the media as the guardian of democracy, the media consist largely of profit-sector enterprises that will continue to behave as such. That means an emphasis on differences among Americans rather than commonalities. The commercial success of the newspapers and news shows depends on good story lines, and conflict is a good story line.[28]

Nevertheless, for the sake of American democracy, the members of the media need to wake up and realize that not everything is about a conflict, about a good story line, about pure profit. Everything is not a show. The work of government that deals with significant domestic and foreign policy issues that affect millions of people in the United States and around the world is not a game. It cannot be responsibly dealt with as a contest, as who wins and who loses or who is up and who is down. It cannot be responsibly dealt with in 6-second sound bites or in a series of shouting matches. And adding more and more voices to the debate, more bloggers, more talk-radio hosts, more outlets does nothing to help the debate.

What is needed instead is some limitation on the media. We do not need many more shouting and emotional voices. Rather, we need fewer, reasoned voices. Ideally, the media, as self-proclaimed guardians of American democracy, should take the lead in fostering thoughtful debate and civil dialogue in the society. But since the media are not likely to do this, perhaps the cameras can be cut off from certain aspects of government. One prescription for reform here could be that Congress should eliminate recorded voting on controversial political issues such as abortion or stem cell research or gay rights so that votes on these issues could not be used against candidates in political campaigns.[29] On such highly charged matters, we could return to voice votes, as it used to be the case before the 1970s. The point is that if the media will not cease its obsessive focus on conflict, perhaps some sources of that conflict can be taken away.

Another area of challenge is the role of social issues in contemporary politics. There is no doubt that social issues, such as abortion or gay rights or stem cell research, are exceedingly important to many Americans. They can indeed be central in one's life. They are, nevertheless, intensely personal; they must not be political. They arouse significant emotions, and are known to often lead to considerable friction among the individuals or the groups involved.

As former Missouri GOP Senator John Danforth has argued,

> In the decade since I left the Senate, American politics has been character-
> ized by two phenomena: the increased activism of the Christian right,
> especially in the Republican Party, and the collapse of bipartisan collegiality.
> I do not think it is a stretch to suggest a relationship between the two.
> To assert that I am on God's side and you are not, that I know God's will
> and you do not, and that I will use the power of government to advance
> my understanding of God's kingdom is certain to produce hostility.[30]

At another place, in *Faith and Politics,* Danforth writes:

> The problem is not that Christians are conservative or liberal, but that some
> are so confident that their position is God's position that they become
> dismissive and intolerant toward others and divisive forces in our national
> life.... The problem of American politics is not the different positions people
> take—disagreeing on positions is the nature of politics. The problem is the
> divisiveness that makes civil discourse, much less reasonable compromise,
> so difficult today. Wedge issues split us apart, and when the wedges are
> driven from two directions at the same time, the split becomes even more
> forbidding.[31]

To Danforth, and to many others, social issues evoke a certain
kind of certainty, resulting in a dislike or even hatred for those with
differing views. To him, perhaps the best way out might be to
take social issues out of government's sphere. When asked about government's involvement, for example, in the issue of gay marriage,
Danforth responded, "It's just cussedness."[32]

Let me echo Danforth's remarks and make a suggestion for the
removal of social issues out of the public square. While these issues
are very important to individuals, the government should adopt a
hands off approach when it comes to them. The fundamental point is
simple: government deals with public matters; these are private
matters. While I have no specific suggestion for how to remove these
issues out of government's arena, I believe that if the two major parties
reverted to how they perceived themselves and the government in the
1950s and the 1960s, focusing on economic and foreign policy matters
and not on social matters, perhaps these issues will begin to be taken
out of electioneering as divisive wedge issues and then out of
governing as well. That is in fact how the parties were and that is

indeed how the government is supposed to be, and for the sake of a healthy American polity, we should return to that.

Finally, and perhaps most significantly, a measure that would go a long way toward minimizing vitriolic behavior and increasing trust in Congress is enhanced interaction among members. There is an almost universal agreement among scholars, pundits, and former members of Congress that if the members got to know each other better, they would be far less likely to engage in name-calling and far less likely to cast dispersions on their colleagues' motives.

Congressman LaHood, the Illinois Republican, drove this point home in his remarks to the Woodstock Report. Speaking at length, he said:

> Another factor [contributing to uncivil behavior] is the way we lead our lives as members of the House of Representatives. The vast majority of the members go back to their home districts every weekend. They board a plane on Thursday afternoon, they go home to their families and their constituents, and come back on Monday or Tuesday. That does not lead you to develop close working relationships with the people you're elected with. While you're in Washington you're running to your committees, which is what I did today. Then I had an office full of people all afternoon from my district who wanted to see me. I'm here this evening. I'll go back to the House tomorrow. We had two votes today, and we'll have a number of votes tomorrow and Thursday. When you multiply that by 435 members who are scurrying all over the Capitol, you may have a chance to say hello to colleagues, but you certainly never have an opportunity to get to know them. Most families live in the home districts; there are very few opportunities for spouses to get to know one another.[33]

He added, "[o]nce you know somebody, it's a lot tougher to criticize them. We are still going to have our partisan differences and spirited debate. But when the debate is over, we ought to be able to walk off the House floor, shake hands, and move on to the next issue."[34]

Former congresswoman Lynn Martin, also a Republican from Illinois, observed in an interview that "the difference [between now and before] is people used to be able to disagree and then get together on other issues, maybe even have dinner or a drink together and be friends. That's what seems to be missing."[35] That is precisely what appears to be missing to nationally noted presidential historian Doris Kearns Goodwin also. She notes,

> I think there was an institutional patriotism when you belonged to the House and the Senate. It was the culmination of your life to be in that job. You spent time in Washington. You didn't run around quite as much in your district because the transportation wasn't as great. So there were friendships that formed, and it was that friendship that, for example, Lyndon Johnson was able to deal with when he needed bipartisan support to get the filibuster ended on civil rights. He could go to Dirksen. He had spent hours with him sitting at night, drinking, swapping stories. He got Hubert Humphrey to go up to the Hill and say, I've courted Dirksen more assiduously than I courted my wife, Muriel. And he made Dirksen feel if you go with me on civil rights and break this southern filibuster, you will be writing a chapter in the history of the Senate, and you will be proud.[36]

To Mann also, the point of socializing with colleagues is not trivial. He observes, "[t]here are plenty of experiences in the House gym, where liberals and conservatives have joined sides in a basketball game. That connection allows them to pull back on the floor of the House, when the ideological instinct was to go for the jugular, and say, 'No! He's on my team!' So, I think that personal experience is terribly important."[37]

A key part of the problem here is scheduling. As George Will has noted, "[t]he House often works Tuesday to Thursday, and many members do not move their families to Washington, so there is less of the socializing that leavens partisanship with friendship."[38]

As Mann and Ornstein have argued,

> Congress should adopt a new schedule, going two weeks on and two weeks off, with the two weeks on beginning early Monday morning and going to late Friday afternoon—in other words, a typical work week and not the Tuesday late afternoon to Thursday early afternoon schedule that has become the norm....That kind of schedule change may sound trivial—it is not. If members were at the Capitol for extended periods, including, most likely, the weekends in between the "on" weeks—they would interact with each other more frequently and more directly, including across party lines, developing interpersonal relationships that are now often nonexistent. Weekends spent in Washington would include more socialization with colleagues and their families and build the kinds of links that used to be commonplace and now are not. It might even encourage more members to bring their families to Washington, adding to the stability of legislating.[39]

Alternatively, Congressman Baird has argued that the House should be in session for three full weeks in a row (five days a week), then take one full week off.[40]

Whatever the particular schedule, though, the notion of remaining in session longer, of remaining in Washington longer than just flying in and out, is an important one. Eilperin writes that Congress should "[f]orce members to stay in town more often...so members can get to know each other and have more flexibility to meet with constituents back home as well as in D.C....By making Democrats and Republicans spend more time together, lawmakers might establish the sort of rapport that often underpins substantive policy accords."[41] The idea of spending more time in Washington and socializing with colleagues is echoed by Billy Tauzin as well. He told Eilperin that "[m]embers need to spend more time socializing with each other...so they can discover redeeming qualities in their partisan opponents."[42]

The Democrats, after they regained majorities in both houses after the 2006 midterm elections, did announce that the House would be open five days a week, rather than have just the Tuesday through Thursday schedule.[43] The new schedule, nonetheless, was excessively short-lived, as it lasted only the opening days of the 110th Congress.

A commitment to a longer work week in the House would be a much-needed reform on the Hill. Spending more time in Washington, ideally spending some weekends their as well, will allow (perhaps even force) members to spend more time with each other. All of this time spent together does not have to be about business, about legislating. Indeed, it is important that it is not. The point is that members need to get to know each other better, they need to socialize with each other's families, they need to build friendships and relationships. That is what is missing on the Hill these days. As everyone agrees, having friendships would mean a better understanding of each other, resulting in less partisan friction and questioning of each other's motives.

My preference in this regard would be to follow Congressman Baird's suggestion. The House should be in session Monday through Friday for three weeks in a row, with one week off. This would be consistent with the Senate's schedule. Moreover, it would perhaps force members to bring their families to Washington since they would have a very limited time to travel back home every weekend and induce more interaction among members. Members can still go home during the off week when the House is not in session to visit their constituents. Such a change in schedule would be a very important reform in the right direction.

Why are trust and civility important? Why is pragmatism important? Pragmatism and civility and trust are vital due to the fact that they are essential qualities on the road to success in the political arena, especially in American politics. It is very important for any politician to remember that politics is about the art of the possible, not the art of the most desirable. It is also equally important for any politician to remember that politics is not about black and white, it is about a whole lot of gray. In this sea of grayness, where neither side is totally right, it is critical to put some faith in the other side. That faith, nevertheless, will not come about with constant name-calling and finger-pointing.

Doris Kearns Goodwin relays the story about James Madison, who was once asked to identify what he thought were the greatest principles of the Constitution. According to Goodwin, Madison responded, "there are three: compromise, compromise, compromise."[44]

The American system of government is not built for ideologues. Were it designed for purists, we would have something more like a parliamentary system of government. Politics as a general rule, but politics especially in the American system of government, is about incremental steps, about getting what one can get today, and leaving the rest for another battle the next day. The focus on what is possible is critical in a free, open, and multicultural society, with a system of government based upon separation of powers and checks and balances and a structure of society replete with pluralistic arrangements.

Politics, thus, in a democratic realm, is very much a balancing act between competing values. As Mann has argued, "[i]n democracies, any of the grand ideological debates involve a choice between competing truths rather than between truth and falsehood: the need to promote risk-taking *and* the need to provide security, the importance of protecting tradition *and* the importance of preserving tolerance, the imperative of personal responsibility *and* the imperative of mutual assistance" (emphasis in original).[45]

It is admittedly awfully tempting for members of Congress, particularly in this era of heightened partisanship, to cling to their ideologies and not want to compromise. It is awfully easy to willfully launch grenades at the other side when they are unable to get their way.

My plea, as I near the end of this book, is for members of Congress to get along. Any other way cannot be a way forward. As I have demonstrated in chapters 5 and 6, getting along is not only good for the institution (the respect for Congress drops when members are excessively partisan or uncivil) but good for the legislative process as well (excessive partisanship and incivility make legislating nearly impossible). These are stark and, in the long run, unacceptable consequences of not getting along. There are significant problems in this country that will not be solved if the present environment of mindless partisanship and high-pitched rhetoric continues. A pragmatic approach, therefore, is terribly needed. Vitally important issues like Social Security changes, the health care reform, immigration reform, to name just a few, cannot be effectively solved with the two sides at each other's throats, with each side thinking only of its immediate electoral advantage. In the global setting, too, internal bickering and finger-pointing presumably threatens the execution of an effective foreign policy.

So what must contemporary politicians do? A prescription for individual members of Congress, in addition to the one for institutional reforms outlined above, might be helpful at this juncture. First and foremost, members of House and Senate need to begin desperately to think more for the long-term than just for the short-term. Every move must not be for the immediate, momentary electoral advantage. Members must think of the institution of Congress, which is a symbol of American democracy. Perhaps a focus on members' legacies, of what they become known for, of what they leave behind, of what great program they helped create, or of what great crisis they helped solve, might push members to think for the long haul. Members must realize that they have been afforded a tremendous privilege to serve in the House or Senate, and they must use that service to leave a name for themselves.

In this focus on the long haul, it does not serve well to shamelessly use the media for one's personal or partisan advantage. Every move is not about a 30-second commercial or a 20-second sound bite. Indeed, to make the kind of hard choices that exceptionally complex issues like Social Security or health care or immigration require, one must deliberately move away from the glare of camera lights. Hard compromises on tough issues cannot be done in the open, where everyone is jockeying for always winning and always looking good. In fact, some of the best and most accomplished legislators in the history of Congress have been those who have shunned the limelight and worked behind the scenes to get things done for the country. The famous former Democratic Speaker of the House Tip O'Neill loved to say, "I'm a back-room operator, no question about it."[46] Modern leaders should remember this.

In order to build a legacy and think for the long-term, members will inevitably have to take on the interest groups from time to time. As discussed above, interest groups exist to serve their own narrow causes. There is no interest group for the United States. As Paul Krugman of the *New York Times* writes,

> [s]ometimes it seems as if Americans have forgotten what courage means. Here's a hint: talking tough doesn't make you a hero; you have to take personal risks. And I'm not just talking about physical risks—though it's striking how few of our biggest flag wavers have ever put themselves in harm's way. What we should demand of our representatives in Washington is the willingness to take political risks—to make a stand on principle, even if it means taking on powerful interest groups.[47]

Above all else, it is exceedingly vital that members of Congress do absolutely whatever they can to stop questioning each other's motives. Tauzin, the former member of the House, has called for enforcing "the rule that prohibits members from questioning one another's motives on the House floor, one that politicians flout constantly."[48] Every member represents a different constituency, comes with a different agenda, and has a personal philosophy of being a member. These differences ought to be respected. There is probably nothing that irks one more than being accused of deception or disingenuousness. Members are influenced by a variety of factors in their jobs and it is imperative that members be taken at their word. No one else can really know what is motivating a particular member on a particular issue. Questioning each other's motives engenders suspicion and distrust and aggravates the already-fragile relationship between the two sides of the aisle.

Of course, in an effort to rebuild long-lasting bridges with members across the aisle, a great deal will have to be done institutionally to restore "regular order" in the House and Senate. Regular order that focuses on fair procedures, giving minority the voice in debate in committees and on the floor and open rules that allow minorities to amend legislation, will go a long way toward reducing the animosity for the other side. Note Mann and Ornstein, "[r]egular order in a legislature—produced by an elaborate set of rules, precedents, and norms governing the conduct of business in committee, on the floor, and in conference—is designed to facilitate orderly and deliberate policy making, ensure fairness, and maintain the legitimacy of Congress and the constitutional system. Majorities are always tempted to dispense with regular order to advance their immediate policy and political objectives."[49] Eilperin advocates opening up the rules process, "so dissenters in both the minority and the majority can amend legislation." She further adds, "[a]llow time for floor debate so members have a chance to exchange ideas, and perhaps sway each other on occasion."[50]

The restoration of regular order is quite likely to be an important step in reestablishing trust in the other side. In addition, it is quite likely to produce better legislation by permitting the minority to fairly participate in the legislative process. Also, it will contribute to a better image of Congress, since it will produce less partisan bickering. The minority, although well protected in the Senate, needs a voice and a shot at amending legislation. The minority, be it Democratic or Republican, needs a sense of the fair play. The minority, as members of the legislative body, needs to know that its opinions are valued and respected, even though it may lose at the end of the day. Just the feelings that its opinions were heard and there was a fair procedure applied will increase friendships and cross-party trust, even if the minority ends up losing on most of the votes. These are important steps toward a more pragmatic Congress.

A good study in pragmatism and comity came recently in the form of the Iraq Study Group. This group contained ten commissioners, five Republicans and five Democrats, charged with evaluating America's role in Iraq. The members, despite representing "a wide range of political backgrounds and philosophical views," spoke highly of their deliberations and seemed to be exceptionally pleased about genuine bipartisanship among themselves. Al Simpson, former Republican senator from Wyoming and a member of the commission, is quoted to have said, "We very quickly stopped considering ourselves as Republicans and Democrats, but as Americans trying to deal with a most urgent problem." Vernon Jordan, a Democratic lawyer and also a commissioner, said, "This process has been a lesson in civility." The members worked hard to reach consensus, and they released their report with unanimous agreement. One of the key ingredients in this success story was that the members bonded together, they socialized with each other. Leon Panetta, a former Democratic member of the House and chief of staff under President Clinton, said of their trip together to Baghdad, "[f]ifteen hours on the plane together and three days in a tough place—that was a human experience where we shared a lot and really got to know each other." Indeed, both Panetta and Simpson, speaking more broadly, wish Congress would follow their example. Said Simpson, "This could be an example, not only of how to handle Iraq, but it could apply to immigration, Social Security and all those other things that have been hung up for so long." Said Panetta, "Our forefathers intended that a process like this work for people elected to office—the president and members of Congress in both the House and Senate. They believed they would come from different places but ultimately find consensus—that was the Miracle of Philadelphia."[51]

Modern politicians must strenuously avoid the constant railing against politics, against compromise, and against government, all for the sake of momentary electoral advantage. As Jim Hoagland has argued, "[t]hat advantage turns out to be temporary and ultimately self-defeating. Related assaults on politics as a profession, on compromise as a function of government and on taxes as a valid instrument for common welfare turn quickly into dead ends. They deliver only instant gratification for the frustrated." This practice is not confined to Washington; it is widely deployed in European capitals as well. It was evident in the rise and fall of public popularity of George Bush, of British Prime Minister Tony Blair, of Italian Prime Minister Silvio Berlusconi, and of French Prime Minister Dominique de Villepin. Such leaders only leave behind a shell. As Hoagland ultimately cautions and prays, "the current popular mood of suspicion and disdain of government—exacerbated by opportunistic or insensitive anti-politicians as well as by an intrusive 24-7 media—risks throwing the baby out with the bath water. The professional politicians who can bring back to Washington a spirit of creative bipartisanship will earn the thanks of a grateful nation."[52]

There are those who believe that comity and institutional respect will only come if the public wants it, if the public demands it. Tauzin maintains, "[t]here is no institutional support for restoring comity and respect and order. It's going to take some cataclysmic voter reaction." In echoing this sentiment, Gephardt has said, "The only way to get back to a more collaborative atmosphere is for the people to demand it. The voters will ultimately judge if they're getting what they want, or what they need."[53] That argument, however, flies in the face of what some, most notably political scientist Uslaner, whose work on this topic has been referenced widely in this book, have noted, that the public itself is less civil and respectful than is used to be. Given the public's sparse attention to politics and its own heightened levels of incivility, the demand for an attitudinal change in Congress is not likely to be spearheaded by the public.

Instead of putting the onus on the public, my take is that members of Congress, as the political elites of this country, need to be grown up about it. They should step up to the plate for the restoration of comity and bipartisanship. In the end, as Mann and Ornstein note, "we must face the reality that even if we could get the procedural, ethics, and electoral reforms through just as we would draft them, and even if we could include serious reform of the committee structure and of the budget process, it would not change Congress dramatically unless and until the leaders of Congress change their approach to governance."[54] It is, therefore, an attitudinal change that members themselves must bring to the table. Perhaps it is the newest members who will bring about this change.[55]

As members of the world's greatest legislative body, representatives and senators must themselves fight for changes in internal mechanisms to ensure fair processes. They must be the ones to show concern for Congress. In the end, to quote Mann and Ornstein once again, "[a] sense of fair play, of balanced rules that cover everybody, and of concern for the very integrity of the institution would go a long way toward restoring confidence in the First Branch."[56]

In the end, it is the members themselves who must show political courage to take on the divisive interest groups, the shortsighted consultants, and the polarizing media. Members must be the very first to stand up for their own institution. As former GOP member from Oklahoma, Mickey Edwards, has said in another context, "[w]hat is needed is serious surgery: the Congress needs a backbone."[57] The onus is on members to show that they can stand up for Congress and that they can stop behaving badly.

Notes

Chapter 1: The Problem of Incivility and Partisanship

1. Cokie Roberts, "A Time When Partisanship Didn't Mean Enmity," broadcast on National Public Radio, January 26, 2007.

2. Lee H. Hamilton, *How Congress Works and Why You Should Care* (Bloomington, IN: Indiana University Press, 2004), 47.

3. Robert B. Reich, *Locked in the Cabinet* (New York: Vintage, 1998), 167.

4. "Civil Discourse and American Politics," *Woodstock Report*, June 1997, no. 50.

5. John McCain, "Address by Senator John McCain to the 2000 Republican National Convention," August 1, 2000.

6. NBC News/Wall Street Journal Poll, April 21–24, 2006.

7. NPR News and the Pew Research Center for the People and the Press, January 10–15, 2007.

8. Thomas E. Mann and Norman J. Ornstein, *The Broken Branch: How Congress Is Failing America and How to Get It Back on Track* (New York: Oxford University Press, 2006), 67.

9. Juliet Eilperin, *Fight Club Politics: How Partisanship Is Poisoning the House of Representatives* (Lanham, MD: Rowman & Littlefield, 2006), 130.

10. Quoted in Keith Perine, "Putting Politics on the Bench," *Congressional Quarterly Weekly Report*, June 12, 2004, 1404.

11. John Cochran, "Frist Sheds Low-Key Style for High-Octane Finish," *Congressional Quarterly Weekly Report*, November 15, 2003; Jennifer A. Dlouhy, "Judicial War Far from Over," *Congressional Quarterly Weekly Report*, November 15, 2003; Gebe Martinez and Keith Perine, "Talkathon a Practice for 2004," *Congressional Quarterly Weekly Report*, November 15, 2003.

12. For detailed cases of how both parties increasingly use "postelectoral" or "nonelectoral" means for political conflict and gamesmanship, see Benjamin Ginsberg and Martin Shefter, *Politics by Other Means: Politicians, Prosecutors, and the Press from Watergate to Whitewater* (New York: W.W. Norton, 1999).

13. Clem Miller, *Member of the House: Letters of a Congressman*, ed. John W. Baker (New York: Scribner, 1962), 93.

14. Quoted in Alan Ehrenhalt, "In the Senate of the '80s, Team Spirit Has Given Way to the Rule of Individuals," *Congressional Quarterly Weekly Report*, September 4, 1982, 2176, 2181.

15. Mann and Ornstein, *The Broken Branch*, 224–26.

16. Ibid., 212–13.

17. Joe Klein, *Politics Lost: How American Democracy Was Trivialized by People Who Think You're Stupid* (New York: Doubleday, 2006), 15.

18. Bill Keller, "America's Most Wanting," *New York Times*, November 2, 2002.

19. "Men of Stature: Archer, Moynihan Elevated Political Life," *Dallas Morning News*, November 8, 2000.

20. A large class, totaling fourteen, that included some of these senators but others as well, left the Senate in 1996. Their extraordinary farewell speeches are printed in Norman J. Ornstein, ed., *Lessons and Legacies* (Reading, MA: Addison Wesley, 1997).

21. A detailed analysis of the shift from moderate to partisan members, including a fuller roster of these members, is presented in chapter 3.

22. Mann and Ornstein, *The Broken Branch*, 211.

23. Eilperin, *Fight Club Politics*, 8–9.

24. Ibid., 6.

25. James Q. Wilson, "Divided We Stand," *Opinion Journal*, February 15, 2006.

26. Donald Matthews, *U.S. Senators and Their World* (New York: Vintage, 1960).

27. See, for instance, Barbara Sinclair, *The Transformation of the U.S. Senate* (Baltimore: Johns Hopkins University Press, 1989); Herbert F. Weisberg, Eric S. Heberlig, and Lisa M. Campoli, "How Do Legislatures Operate?" in *Classics in Congressional Politics*, ed. Herbert F. Weisberg, Eric S. Heberlig, and Lisa M. Campoli (New York: Longman, 1999).

28. Hugh Heclo, "Campaigning and Governing: A Conspectus," in *The Permanent Campaign and Its Future*, ed. Norman J. Ornstein and Thomas E. Mann (Washington, D.C.: American Enterprise Institute and Brookings Institution, 2000).

29. Eric M. Uslaner, *The Decline of Comity in Congress* (Ann Arbor: University of Michigan Press, 1993), chap. 3.

30. Congressman Dan Miller presented these in a talk entitled "How Will Congress Respond to the Twenty-First Century" at the Ray C. Bliss Institute of Applied Politics, The University of Akron, February 4, 2004. Congressman Miller served in the House from Florida from 1992 to 2002.

31. Lee H. Hamilton, "A Responsibility for Civility," *State Legislatures*, January 2005, 19.

32. Christopher R. Darr, "Civility as Rhetorical Enactment: The John Ashcroft 'Debates' and Burke's Theory of Form," *Southern Communication Journal* 70, no. 4 (2005): 318.

33. Kathleen Hall Jamieson, "Civility in the House of Representatives," The Annenberg Public Policy Center, University of Pennsylvania, APPC Report #10, March 1997.

34. Television interview on NBC's "Meet the Press," December 24, 2006.

35. "Why Civility Matters," *Des Moines Register,* July 6, 2004.

36. Statement of Eric M. Uslaner, "Civility in the House of Representatives," Subcommittee on Rules and Organization, House Rules Committee, April 17, 1997.

37. Eric M. Uslaner, "Is the Senate More Civil than the House?" in *Esteemed Colleagues: Civility and Deliberation in the U.S. Senate,* ed. Burdett A. Loomis (Washington, D.C.: Brookings Institution Press, 2000), 34.

38. DeAlva Stanwood Alexander, *History and Procedures of the House of Representatives* (Boston: Houghton Mifflin, 1916); William Parkes Cutler and Julia Perkins Cutler, eds., *Life, Journals and Correspondence of the Reverend Manasseh Cutler* (Cincinnati: Robert Clark and Co., 1888); Bernard Mayo, *Henry Clay: Spokesman of the New West* (Boston: Houghton Mifflin, 1937).

39. Alexander, *History and Procedures,* 115–16.

40. Mann and Ornstein, *The Broken Branch,* 242.

41. Uslaner, *The Decline of Comity in Congress;* Loomis, ed., *Esteemed Colleagues;* and Colton C. Campbell and Nicol C. Rae, eds., *The Contentious Senate: Partisanship, Ideology, and the Myth of Cool Judgment* (Lanham, MD: Rowman & Littlefield, 2001).

Chapter 2: The Capitol Hill Junior High School

1. William F. Clinger, "Clinger Says Congress Lacks Civility," *Chautauquan Daily,* July 20, 2001, 4.

2. "Civil Discourse," Online NewsHour, interview transcript, January 30, 1997.

3. Diane Granat, "The House's TV War: The Gloves Come Off," *Congressional Quarterly Weekly Report,* May 19, 1984, 1166–67.

4. "Republicans Protest Recount of Indiana Vote," *New York Times,* April 26, 1985, B20.

5. *Congressional Record,* Daily Edition, 99th Congress, 1st session, April 23, 1985, H2650; *Congressional Record,* Daily Edition, 99th Congress, 1st session, May 1, 1985, H2775.

6. David Rapp, "The Indiana Parable," *Congressional Quarterly Weekly Report,* July 19, 2003, 1798.

7. Margaret Shapiro, "California Congressman Puts on a Floor Show," *Washington Post,* June 20, 1985, A3.

8. Rowland Evans and Robert Novak, "The Kemp-Michel Row," *Washington Post,* April 1, 1987, A23.

9. Janet Hook, "Passion, Defiance, Tears: Jim Wright Bows Out," *Congressional Quarterly Weekly Report,* June 3, 1989, 1289–94; Chuck Alston, "Smear Tactics

Overshadow Election of New Speaker," *Congressional Quarterly Weekly Report*, June 10, 1989, 1373–75.

10. Tom Kenworthy, "On Hill, 'Nothing Is Funny Anymore,'" *Washington Post*, October 18, 1990, A25, A32.

11. William S. Cohen, *Roll Call: One Year in the United States Senate* (New York: Simon and Schuster, 1981), 238.

12. James A. Miller, *Running in Place: Inside the Senate* (New York: Simon and Schuster, 1986), 135.

13. Quoted in Barbara Sinclair, *The Transformation of the U.S. Senate* (Baltimore: The Johns Hopkins University Press, 1989), 99.

14. For the record, it should be written that Dole was exceedingly compromising and bipartisan in many of his dealings with his colleagues, both Democrats and Republicans. While he may have acquired a reputation for being mean-spirited and acerbic in his rhetoric, Dole was nothing but graceful in his farewell address to the Senate, praising those whom he had served with, perhaps even being laudatory of more Democrats than Republicans.

15. *Congressional Record*, Daily Edition, 101st Congress, 1st session, March 7, 1989, S2241.

16. Helen Dewar, "Suspicions Simmer in the Senate," *Washington Post*, July 22, 1990, A16.

17. Guy Gugliotta, "Taking Decorum Down," *Washington Post*, January 2, 1996, A13.

18. Associated Press, "Cunningham Apologizes for Curse, Gesture, Crude Remark," *Washington Post*, September 8, 1998, A6.

19. Senator Alfonse D'Amato, *Power, Pasta, and Politics* (New York: Hyperion, 1995), 140–48.

20. Representative James A. Leach, "A Call for a Renewed Sense of Civility in Public Life," The Bowen Lecture, The University of Iowa, Iowa City, Iowa, November 29, 2000, 7.

21. Ibid.

22. Ibid.

23. Eric Planin and Juliet Eilperin, "No Love Lost for Hastert, Gephardt," *Washington Post*, March 20, 2000, A4.

24. Karen Foerstel, "Hastert and the Limits of Persuasion," *Congressional Quarterly Weekly Report*, September 30, 2000, 2252–54.

25. Ibid., 2254.

26. Eric Schmitt, "When Senators Attack," *New York Times*, June 11, 2000, WK7; *Congressional Record*, May 17, 2000, S4067–69.

27. *Congressional Record*, May 17, 2000, S4067–69.

28. Lizette Alvarez and Eric Schmitt, "Undignified and Screaming, Senate Seeks to Right Itself," *New York Times*, June 7, 2000, A26.

29. Gugliotta, "Taking Decorum Down."

30. Robin Toner, "Angry Opposition Attacks the Process," *New York Times,* September 22, 1995, A26.

31. Gugliotta, "Taking Decorum Down."

32. Toner, "Angry Opposition Attacks the Process."

33. David Nather, "Contrite Chairman Does Not Quell Calls for More GOP Comity," *Congressional Quarterly Weekly Report,* July 26, 2003, 1888.

34. Senator Mitch McConnell, "Functioning of the Senate," *Congressional Record,* November 10, 2003, S14286.

35. Senator Rick Santorum, *Congressional Record,* November 12, 2003, S14683.

36. Dlouhy, "Judicial War Far from Over," 2826.

37. Senator Tom Daschle, "Farewell," *Congressional Record,* November 19, 2004, S11559.

38. Dana Milbank and Helen Dewar, "Cheney Defends Use of Four-Letter Word," *Washington Post,* June 26, 2004, A4.

39. Ibid.

40. James P. Pfiffner, "Partisan Polarization, Politics, and the Presidency," in *Rivals for Power: Presidential-Congressional Relations,* ed. James A. Thurber, 3rd ed. (Lanham, MD: Rowman & Littlefield, 2006), 43.

41. Quoted in John J. Pitney, Jr., "The War on the Floor: Partisan Conflict in the U.S. House of Representatives," paper presented at the 1988 annual meeting of the American Political Science Association, Washington, D.C.

42. Geoff Earle, "Rangel & Veep in All-Out War," *New York Post,* October 31, 2006.

43. Ibid.

44. "Senate Leader Calls Bush 'A Loser,'" CBS News, May 7, 2005.

45. Tony Batt, "Reid Doesn't Back Down from Friday Remark about Bush," *Las Vegas Review-Journal,* May 11, 2005.

46. Senator Harry Reid, "Reid: Republicans Cannot Be Trusted to End the Culture of Corruption," Senator Reid's Senate Web site, January 17, 2006.

47. Senator Harry Reid, "Reid Addresses the Real State of Our Union," Senator Reid's Senate Web site, January 24, 2006.

48. Carl Hulse and Jeff Zeleny, "Bush and Cheney Chide Democrats on Iraq Deadline," *New York Times,* April 25, 2007.

49. "Hillary Clinton Blasts GOP 'Plantation,'" The Associated Press, January 16, 2006.

50. Mary Snow and Candy Crowley, "Clinton's 'Plantation' Remark Draws Fire," CNN.com, January 17, 2006. It should be noted that the "plantation" remark has been used by other congressional leaders before. As Snow and Crowley report, former Speaker Gingrich, before taking over the House of Representatives in 1994, said that the Democrats "think it's their job to run the plantation" and that "it shocks them that I'm actually willing to lead the slave rebellion."

51. Laurie Kellman, "Feingold, Specter Clash Over Gay Marriage," *Washington Post,* May 18, 2006.

52. Michael D. Shear, "In Following His Own Script, Webb May Test Senate's Limits," *Washington Post*, November 29, 2006, A01.

53. Senator Robert Byrd, "Civility in the Senate," *Congressional Record*, December 20, 1995, S18964–S19871.

54. Juliet Eilperin, "Comity Hour with Mike Mansfield," *Washington Post*, March 25, 1998, A19.

55. Ibid.

Chapter 3: Changing of the Guard

1. John Danforth, *Faith and Politics: How the "Moral Values" Debate Divides America and How to Move Forward Together* (New York: Viking, 2006), 5–6.

2. It should be noted that these lists are not exclusive by any means. Many others would fit the mold in both groups. These members are simply the leading, publicly known representations of the two eras.

3. Charles L. Clapp, *The Congressman: His Work as He Sees It* (Washington, D.C.: Brookings Institution, 1963), 12–13.

4. Donald R. Matthews, *U.S. Senators and Their World* (New York: Vintage, 1960), see esp. chap. V.

5. "Administration, Republican Reactions to 1967 Session," 1967 Congressional Quarterly Almanac, 95.

6. Ibid.

7. Hamilton, *How Congress Works*, 98–100.

8. Party unity scores were taken from the Congressional Quarterly Almanacs from 1950 to 2000.

9. Nicol C. Rae, *Conservative Reformers: The Republican Freshmen and the Lessons of the 104th Congress* (Armonk, NY: M. E. Sharpe, 1998), 20.

10. Lee Hamilton, "Why We Need Compromise," Comments on Congress, The Center on Congress at Indiana University, May 5, 2003; Lee Hamilton, "Congressional Bickering," Comments on Congress, The Center on Congress at Indiana University, April 11, 2003.

11. Sam Donaldson, *This Week with David Brinkley*, October 10, 1993.

12. Cokie Roberts, *This Week with David Brinkley*, October 10, 1993.

13. Jonathan Allen, "John Rhodes, House GOP Leader Noted for Advising Nixon to Quit, Dies of Cancer at Age 86," *Congressional Quarterly Weekly Report*, August 30, 2003, 2099.

14. Robin Toner, "Southern Democrats' Decline Is Eroding the Political Center," *New York Times*, November 15, 2004.

15. E.J. Dionne, Jr., "Last of a Republican Kind?" *Washington Post*, March 19, 1999, A29.

16. John C. Danforth, "In the Name of Politics," *New York Times*, March 30, 2005, A17.

17. Peter Slevin, "'St. Jack' and the Bullies in the Pulpit," *Washington Post*, February 2, 2006, C01.

18. Warren B. Rudman, "This Isn't Much Fun," *Washington Post Magazine*, April 21, 1996.

19. John Cranford and Allison Stevens, "Former Sen. Moynihan Dies at 76; Colleagues Laud a Unique Voice," *Congressional Quarterly Weekly Report*, March 29, 2003, 758.

20. Ibid.

21. George F. Will, "Farewell, Mr. Moynihan," *Washington Post*, September 17, 2000, B07.

22. Norman J. Ornstein, "Introduction," in *Lessons and Legacies: Farewell Addresses from the Senate*, ed. Norman J. Ornstein (Reading, MA: Addison-Wesley, 1997), xi.

23. Dr. Barry C. Black, "Prayer," *Congressional Record*, November 10, 2003, S14285.

24. It is true that some members who occasionally practice new-style politics were elected to Congress, first on the Senate side, beginning in the late 1950s and 1960s. These included senators like Abraham Ribicoff of Connecticut, Edward Kennedy of Massachusetts, George McGovern of South Dakota, Gaylord Nelson of Wisconsin, and Walter Mondale of Minnesota. However, these were northern liberal Democrats who simply wanted to wrest control and agenda from the southern conservative Democrats. The firebrand new-style members, both on the Democratic and on the Republican sides, were in fact elected first to the House after Watergate, and some migrated to the Senate after a few terms in the House. These included people like Bob Walker of Pennsylvania, Bob Dornan of California, Dan Burton of Indiana, David Bonior of Michigan, Trent Lott of Mississippi, and Rick Santorum of Pennsylvania. The Republican members were trained in the Gingrich school of "slash and burn" politics.

25. George Condon, White House reporter, Copley News Service, C-SPAN's *Journalists' Roundtable*, October 8, 1993.

26. Helen Dewar, "Recasting the Senate as Great Guerrilla Theater," *Washington Post*, May 30, 2000.

27. Quoted in George C. Edwards III, Martin P. Wattenberg, and Robert L. Lineberry, *Government in America: People, Politics, and Policy* (New York: Longman, 2002).

28. Quoted in Michael Barone and Richard E. Cohen, *The Almanac of American Politics 2002* (Washington, D.C.: National Journal, 2001), 578.

29. Keller, "America's Most Wanting."

30. Lou Dubose and Jan Reid, *The Hammer* (Boulder, CO: The Perseus Books Group, 2004).

31. Jonathan Allen, "Tom DeLay, R-Texas," *Congressional Quarterly Weekly Report*, April 3, 2004, 794.

32. Keller, "America's Most Wanting."

33. "Heights of Arrogance," *USA Today,* April 5, 2006, 11A.

34. Rae, *Conservative Reformers,* 20–21.

35. Mann and Ornstein, *The Broken Branch,* 65.

36. Barone and Cohen, *Almanac of American Politics 2002,* 251.

37. Uslaner, *The Decline of Comity in Congress,* 33.

38. Barone and Cohen, *Almanac of American Politics 2002,* 1131.

39. Quoted in ibid.

40. Shawn Zeller, "Inhofe's Kiss-Off," *Congressional Quarterly Weekly Report,* January 16, 2006, 159.

41. Keller, "America's Most Wanting."

42. Quoted in Nicol C. Rae and Colton C. Campbell, "Party Politics and Ideology in the Contemporary Senate," in *The Contentious Senate: Partisanship, Ideology, and the Myth of Cool Judgment,* ed. Colton C. Campbell and Nicol C. Rae (Lanham, MD: Rowman & Littlefield, 2001), 13.

43. Quoted in Dewar, "Recasting the Senate as Great Guerrilla Theater."

44. Barone and Cohen, *Almanac of American Politics 2002,* 859.

45. Allison Stevens, "Sen. Nickles Will Be Remembered More for What He Fought Against," *Congressional Quarterly Weekly Report,* October 11, 2003, 2497–99.

46. Kevin Merida, "The Freshman Who Raised the Fuss; Santorum Hopes Hatfield Episode Sends a Message to GOP Leadership," *Washington Post,* March 9, 1995, A27.

47. Norman J. Ornstein, "Civility, Deliberation, and Impeachment," in *Esteemed Colleagues: Civility and Deliberation in the U.S. Senate,* ed. Burdett A. Loomis (Washington, D.C.: Brookings Institution Press, 2000), 239.

48. Senator Strom Thurmond's career low of 15 for party unity came early in his Senate career when he was a Democrat. After he switched to the GOP, he was a strong Republican partisan.

Chapter 4: What Is Behind Partisanship and Uncivil Debate in Congress?

1. Senator William S. Cohen, in Ornstein, *Lessons and Legacies,* 46.

2. National Election Studies, *The NES Guide to Public Opinion and Electoral Behavior, 1952–2000,* table 20.1.

3. James Q. Wilson and John J. DiIulio, Jr., *American Government: The Essentials,* 9th ed. (Boston: Houghton Mifflin, 2004), 162.

4. Morris Fiorina, *Divided Government,* 2nd ed. (Boston: Allyn and Bacon, 1996), 6.

5. Uslaner, *The Decline of Comity in Congress,* 52.

6. Paul S. Herrnson, *Congressional Elections: Campaigning at Home and in Washington,* 4th ed. (Washington, D.C.: Congressional Quarterly, 2004), 6–7.

7. Gary C. Jacobson, *The Politics of Congressional Elections*, 5th ed. (New York: Addison Wesley Longman, 2001), 57.

8. Ibid., 5.

9. Anthony King, *Running Scared: Why America's Politicians Campaign Too Much and Govern Too Little* (New York: The Free Press, 1997), 38–39.

10. David S. Broder, "Gutless Government," *Washington Post Weekly*, November 6, 1989, 4.

11. Norman J. Ornstein, Thomas E. Mann, and Michael J. Malbin, *Vital Statistics on Congress 2001–2002* (Washington, D.C.: The American Enterprise Institute Press, 2002), 75. Some political scientists draw the benchmark for electoral safety at 55 percent, in which case these figures would be even higher.

12. Eilperin, *Fight Club Politics*, 97.

13. Mann and Ornstein, *The Broken Branch*, 12.

14. Ibid.

15. Quoted in Roger H. Davidson and Walter J. Oleszek, *Congress and Its Members*, 9th ed. (Washington, D.C.: Congressional Quarterly, 2004), 209.

16. Ibid.

17. Martin P. Wattenberg, "From a Partisan to a Candidate-Centered Electorate," in *The New American Political System*, ed. Anthony King, 2nd ed. (Washington, D.C.: American Enterprise Institute, 1990), 156.

18. Ibid.

19. Kay Lehman Schlozman and John T. Tierney, *Organized Interests and American Democracy* (New York: Harper and Row, 1986), 75–76.

20. As a related matter, these congressional reforms also often get cited as another cause of the increased vitriol in Congress in recent decades. But, even those who consider them, such as Uslaner does, mention that they are peripheral, rather than central, to increased incivility. According to his analysis, "[c]hanges in institutional design did not directly cause the heightened decibel level in the Congress. The impact was more circuitous, through reciprocity.... At most, reform expedited the avalanche of participation that would have come anyway" (Uslaner, *The Decline of Comity in Congress*, 46–48).

21. Allan J. Cigler and Burdett A. Loomis, "Contemporary Interest Group Politics: More Than 'More of the Same,'" in *Interest Group Politics*, ed. Allan J. Cigler and Burdett A. Loomis, 4th ed. (Washington, D.C.: Congressional Quarterly, 1995), 404.

22. Ibid., 404–5.

23. Mark J. Rozell and Clyde Wilcox, *Interest Groups in American Campaigns* (Washington, D.C.: Congressional Quarterly, 1999), 148.

24. Ibid., 147–48.

25. Wilson, "Divided We Stand."

26. Ibid.

27. Klein, *Politics Lost*, 14.

28. Leroy N. Rieselbach, *Congressional Reform: The Changing Modern Congress* (Washington, D.C.: Congressional Quarterly, 1994), 58.

29. Lyndsey Layton and Jonathan Weisman, "GOP Expects Defections as House Debates Iraq Resolution," *Washington Post,* February 12, 2007, A05.

30. Mann and Ornstein, *The Broken Branch,* 66.

31. Ibid., 66–67.

32. Ronald D. Elving, "Brighter Lights, Wider Windows: Presenting Congress in the 1990s," in *Congress, the Press, and the Public,* ed. Thomas E. Mann and Norman J. Ornstein (Washington, D.C.: American Enterprise Institute and The Brookings Institution, 1994), 178–79.

33. Ibid., 192.

34. Todd Gitlin, "Deliberation in Democracy," *Hedgehog Review: Critical Reflections on Contemporary Culture* 6, no. 3 (2004): 10.

35. "Civil Discourse and American Politics."

36. Wilson, "Divided We Stand."

37. Ibid.

38. Morris P. Fiorina, with Samuel J. Abrams and Jeremy C. Pope, *Culture War? The Myth of a Polarized America* (New York: Pearson Longman, 2006), 3.

39. Klein, *Politics Lost,* 16–17.

40. Herrnson, *Congressional Elections,* 75.

41. Ibid., 69.

42. Larry J. Sabato, *The Rise of Political Consultants* (New York: Basic Books, 1981), 8.

43. Ibid., 5–6.

44. Ibid., 3–7.

45. Mike Barnicle, "Get Consultants Out of the Way," *Boston Globe,* October 25, 1994, 21.

46. Ibid.

47. Stephen K. Medvic, *Political Consultants in U.S. Congressional Elections* (Columbus, OH: Ohio State University Press, 2001), 156.

48. Based upon Sidney Blumenthal's characterization, Hugh Heclo defines permanent campaign as "a combination of image making and strategic calculation that turns governing into a perpetual campaign and 'remakes government into an instrument designed to sustain an elected official's popularity.'" See Hugh Heclo, "Campaigning and Governing: A Conspectus," in *The Permanent Campaign and Its Future,* ed. Norman J. Ornstein and Thomas E. Mann (Washington, D.C.: American Enterprise Institute and The Brookings Institution, 2000), 2.

49. Jim Wright, "The Search for Bipartisanship from Eisenhower to Clinton," The Political Communication Center Lecture Series, University of Oklahoma, November 15, 1994, 23.

50. John Cochran, "For a GOP Congress, Power Begins in the Oval Office," *Congressional Quarterly Weekly Report,* June 12, 2004, 1401.

51. Jim Abrams, "Lawmakers Attempt to Make House More Civil," *Akron Beacon Journal,* February 24, 2005, A8.

52. David S. Broder, "When Partisan Venom Didn't Rule," *Washington Post,* January 29, 2006, B07.

53. "Civil Discourse and American Politics."

54. Ibid.

55. John Cochran, "Disorder in the House—And No End in Sight," *Congressional Quarterly Weekly Report,* April 3, 2004, 790–97.

56. See David S. Broder, "'Center Aisle' Civility," *Washington Post,* December 11, 2005, B07.

Chapter 5: Whither Confidence and Respect in the Modern Congress?

1. Senator J. James Exon, in Ornstein, *Lessons and Legacies,* 57–58.

2. E.J. Dionne, Jr., *Why Americans Hate Politics* (New York: Simon and Schuster, 1991), 11.

3. Ibid., 14–15.

4. Ibid., 332.

5. Ibid., 323.

6. Lawrence C. Dodd, "Congress and the Politics of Renewal: Redressing the Crisis of Legitimation," in *Congress Reconsidered,* ed. Lawrence C. Dodd and Bruce I. Oppenheimer, 5th ed. (Washington, D.C.: Congressional Quarterly, 1993), 418.

7. Ibid., 424.

8. Ibid., 430.

9. David C. King, "The Polarization of American Parties and Mistrust of Government," in *Why People Don't Trust Government,* ed. Joseph S. Nye, Jr., Philip D. Zelikow, and David C. King (Cambridge, MA: Harvard University Press, 1997), 156.

10. Ibid., 178.

11. Ibid., 173–74.

12. Hamilton, *How Congress Works,* 81.

13. The ideology data in Table 5.4 range from –0.5 to 0.5, with –0.5 representing the most extreme Democrats and 0.5 representing the most extreme Republicans. A negative score stands for liberalism and a positive score stands for conservatism, with scores closer to zero standing for centrism and moderation.

14. Diana C. Mutz and Byron Reeves, "The New Videomalaise: Effects of Televised Incivility on Political Trust," *American Political Science Review* 99, no. 1 (2005): 13.

15. Ibid., 12.

16. King, "Polarization of American Parties," 175.

17. Ibid., 176.

18. Ibid., 177.

19. Gary Orren, "Fall from Grace: The Public's Loss of Faith in Government," in *Why People Don't Trust Government*, ed. Joseph S. Nye, Jr., Philip D. Zelikow, and David C. King (Cambridge, MA: Harvard University Press, 1997), 96.

20. John R. Hibbing and Elizabeth Theiss-Morse, *Congress as Public Enemy: Public Attitudes Toward American Political Institutions* (New York: Cambridge University Press, 1995), 54.

21. Ibid., 58.

22. Ibid., 64.

23. Ibid., 145.

24. John R. Hibbing, "Do Americans Care About and Trust Their Government?" *Congressional Briefing*, July 16, 1999, 7.

25. Roger H. Davidson, David M. Kovenock, and Michael O'Leary, *Congress in Crisis: Politics and Congressional Reform* (Belmont, CA: Wadsworth, 1968), 52–53.

26. Roger H. Davidson, "Congress and Public Trust: Is Congress Its Own Worst Enemy?" in *Congress and the Decline of Public Trust*, ed. Joseph Cooper (Boulder, CO: Westview, 1999), 70.

27. Ibid., 71.

28. Ibid., 72.

29. Kenneth R. Mayer and David T. Canon, *The Dysfunctional Congress?: The Individual Roots of an Institutional Dilemma* (Boulder, CO: Westview, 1999), 17.

30. Robert J. Samuelson, "How Polarization Sells," *Washington Post*, June 30, 2004, A21.

31. Senator Bill Bradley, "Foreword: Trust and Democracy: Causes and Consequences of Mistrust of Government," in *Congress and the Decline of Public Trust*, ed. Joseph Cooper (Boulder, CO: Westview, 1999), xii.

Chapter 6: The Impact of Partisan Warfare on the Legislative Process

1. Senator Howell Heflin, in Ornstein, *Lessons and Legacies*, 79–80.

2. Hamilton, "Why We Need Compromise."

3. Hamilton, "A Responsibility for Civility," 19.

4. Senator Robert Dole, "Farewell Address of Senator Robert J. Dole," *Congressional Record*, June 11, 1996, S6044.

5. Gregory A. Caldeira and Samuel C. Patterson, "Political Friendship in the Legislature," *Journal of Politics* 49 (1987): 954.

6. Ross K. Baker, *Friend and Foe in the U.S. Senate* (Acton, MA: Copley, 1999), 21–45.

7. Ibid., 7, 31.

8. Ibid., 294.

9. Ibid., 321–22.

10. Although Baker's study is about the U.S. Senate, and so much of the evidence is from the Senate, he repeatedly points out that the same hypothesis essentially applies to the U.S. House as well.

11. Quoted in Andrew Taylor, "A Different Sense of Urgency," *Congressional Quarterly Weekly Report,* September 30, 2000, 2256.

12. Robert W. Merry, "Senate and Sensibility," *Congressional Quarterly Weekly Report,* May 9, 2005, 1188.

13. Dan Balz, "Bipartisan Group Seeks Own Course on Nominees," *Washington Post,* May 20, 2005, A01.

14. Ibid.

15. Charles Babington, "Senate's 'Gang of 12' Steps In Where Party Leaders Couldn't Go," *Washington Post,* May 20, 2005, A05.

16. Ibid.

17. David Brooks, "Let's Make a Deal," *New York Times,* May 1, 2005, 14.

18. Ibid.

19. David Nather, "Race Against the Nuclear Clock," *Congressional Quarterly Weekly Report,* May 30, 2005, 1440.

20. David Nather, "The Centrists Strike Back," *Congressional Quarterly Weekly Report,* May 30, 2005, 1422.

21. Seth Stern, "Deconstructing the Deal," *Congressional Quarterly Weekly Report,* May 30, 2005, 1443.

22. David S. Broder, "United in Division," *Washington Post,* January 26, 2006, A25.

23. Robin Toner, "Demands of Partisanship Bring Change to the Senate," *New York Times,* May 20, 2005.

24. John Cochran and Gregory L. Giroux, "An End to Senate Strife Unlikely No Matter the Election Outcome," *Congressional Quarterly Weekly Report,* September 18, 2004, 2155–58.

25. John Cochran, "Stalemate Still Lurking in Senate Despite Leaders' Cautious Deals," *Congressional Quarterly Weekly Report,* April 10, 2004, 855.

26. Quoted in Eilperin, *Fight Club Politics,* 52.

27. Ibid., 54.

28. George F. Will, "Why Filibusters Should Be Allowed," *Washington Post,* March 20, 2005, B07.

29. Taylor, "A Different Sense of Urgency," 2256.

30. Cochran, "Stalemate Still Lurking," 856.

31. Jonathan Allen and John Cochran, "The Might of the Right," *Congressional Quarterly Weekly Report,* November 8, 2003, 2761.

32. Ibid., 2762.

33. Eilperin, *Fight Club Politics*, 62–63.

34. Allen and Cochran, "The Might of the Right," 2762.

35. Quoted in Eilperin, *Fight Club Politics*, 47–48.

36. Ibid., 53.

37. Quoted in ibid., 54–55.

38. David S. Broder, "Contempt for Congress," *Washington Post*, August 8, 2006, A21.

39. Allen and Cochran, "The Might of the Right," 2762.

40. In addition, Eilperin reports in *Fight Club Politics* (55–56, 66) that the GOP leadership is now bypassing the rules that give members 48 hours to examine bills before voting by asking the Rules Committee to adopt "emergency" procedures, waiving the 48-hour rule. During the 108th Congress, "[s]ixty percent of all rules qualified for this emergency treatment, and nearly 40 percent of all rules were reported after eight o'clock at night, making it harder for members to examine and propose changes to pending bills before the leadership shepherds the bills to the floor." In 2005, GOP leaders gave Democrats one hour before voting on a 3,000-page, $1 trillion spending bill. Also, GOP leaders are forcing passage of important and controversial bills in the middle of the night, when no one is watching. The famous Medicare vote in 2003 took place between 3 and 6 in the morning, lasted an unprecedented 2 hours and 51 minutes, and passed barely by a vote of 220 to 215 after major-league hardball tactics. Earlier in 2003, a major tax cut measure passed at 1:56 a.m., a bill to cut Head Start funding at 12:57 a.m., and a bill to approve $87 billion for the Iraq war at 12:12 a.m.

41. Quoted in Eilperin, *Fight Club Politics*, 55.

42. Mann and Ornstein, *The Broken Branch*, 242.

43. Ibid.

44. Massimo Calabresi and Perry Bacon, Jr., "America's 10 Best Senators," *Time*, April 24, 2006, 32.

45. Ruth Marcus, "Tyrannosaurus Ted?" *Washington Post*, April 25, 2006, A23.

46. Calabresi and Bacon, Jr., "America's 10 Best Senators," 28.

47. Ibid., 35.

48. Merry, "Senate and Sensibility," 1188.

49. John Cochran, "A Celebrity Senator Moving to the Democratic Center," *Congressional Quarterly Weekly Report*, June 21, 2003, 1525.

50. Martin Kady II, "New York Role, National Stage," *Congressional Quarterly Weekly Report*, April 3, 2006, 908–9.

51. Quoted in Cochran, "A Celebrity Senator Moving to the Democratic Center," 1526.

52. David S. Broder, "Ways and Means—and a Price," *Washington Post*, March 9, 2006, A19.

53. Ibid.

Chapter 7: Democracy Is a Conversation

1. Eilperin, *Fight Club Politics,* 30–37.

2. "Introduction: Discourse and Democracy," *Hedgehog Review: Critical Reflections on Contemporary Culture* 6, no. 3 (2004): 5–6.

3. Christopher McKnight Nichols, "What Would the Public Think?: An Experiment in Deliberative Democracy," *Hedgehog Review: Critical Reflections on Contemporary Culture* 6, no. 3 (2004): 67–68.

4. "Civil Discourse and American Politics."

5. Quoted in ibid.

6. "Civil Discourse and American Politics."

7. E.J. Dionne, Jr., "Beyond the War Spin," *Washington Post,* December 13, 2005, A27.

8. Norman J. Ornstein, "Deliberative Democracy Headed for the 'Dark Side?'" *American Political Science Association (APSA) Legislative Studies Section Newsletter,* 23, no. 2 (2000): 11, 12.

9. Gitlin, "Deliberation in Democracy," 12, 8.

10. David Brooks, "A Polarized America," *Hedgehog Review: Critical Reflections on Contemporary Culture* 6, no. 3 (2004): 16.

11. Fiorina, with Abrams and Pope, *Culture War?* 209.

12. Mann and Ornstein, *The Broken Branch,* 229.

13. Ibid., 230.

14. Eilperin, *Fight Club Politics,* 120.

15. Ibid., 121.

16. Thomas E. Mann, "Redistricting Reform," *National Voter,* June 2005, 5.

17. Ibid., 4–5.

18. Ibid., 6.

19. Eilperin, *Fight Club Politics,* chap. 6.

20. Fiorina, with Abrams and Pope, *Culture War?* 218–19.

21. William E. Brock, "A Recipe for Incivility," *Washington Post,* June 27, 2004, B07.

22. Quoted in Eilperin, *Fight Club Politics,* 125.

23. John Cochran, "A Government Out of Touch," *Congressional Quarterly Weekly Report,* July 4, 2005, 1804–5, 1807.

24. John Cochran, "No Room to Move," *Congressional Quarterly Weekly Report,* May 16, 2005, 1293–98.

25. Fiorina, with Abrams and Pope, *Culture War?* 206.

26. Ornstein, "Deliberative Democracy Headed for the 'Dark Side?'" 12.

27. Ibid., 13.

28. Fiorina, with Abrams and Pope, *Culture War?* 208–9.

29. I owe this suggestion to former Congressman Michael Parker (R-MS), who served in the House from 1988 to 1998. He made this suggestion at a talk entitled

"Congress, Civility and Compromise—Is It Possible?" at the Ray C. Bliss Institute of Applied Politics, The University of Akron, February 7, 2007.

30. John C. Danforth, "Onward, Moderate Christian Soldiers," *New York Times,* June 17, 2005, A27.

31. Danforth, *Faith and Politics,* 10–11.

32. Quoted in Slevin, "'St. Jack' and the Bullies in the Pulpit," C01.

33. "Civil Discourse and American Politics."

34. Ibid.

35. "Civil Discourse."

36. Ibid.

37. "Civil Discourse and American Politics."

38. George F. Will, "How Speaker Pelosi Could Restore Congressional Values," *Newsweek,* December 4, 2006.

39. Mann and Ornstein, *The Broken Branch,* 232.

40. Eilperin, *Fight Club Politics,* 128.

41. Ibid., 128–29.

42. Ibid., 128.

43. Lyndsey Layton, "Culture Shock on Capitol Hill: House to Work 5 Days a Week," *Washington Post,* December 6, 2006, A01.

44. "Civil Discourse."

45. "Civil Discourse and American Politics."

46. Quoted in Alan Ehrenhalt, "Media, Power Shifts Dominate O'Neill's House," *Congressional Quarterly Weekly Report,* September 13, 1986, 2132.

47. Paul Krugman, "For the People," *New York Times,* October 29, 2002.

48. Eilperin, *Fight Club Politics,* 128.

49. Mann and Ornstein, *The Broken Branch,* 215–16.

50. Eilperin, *Fight Club Politics,* 128.

51. David S. Broder, "A Study in Comity," *Washington Post,* December 6, 2006, A25.

52. Jim Hoagland, "The Toll of the Anti-Politicians," *Washington Post,* May 7, 2006, B07.

53. Quoted in Eilperin, *Fight Club Politics,* 136.

54. Mann and Ornstein, *The Broken Branch,* 238–39.

55. See Broder, "'Center Aisle' Civility;" David S. Broder, "Freshmen in the Vital Center," *Washington Post National Weekly Edition,* January 17–23, 2005, 4; Representative Shelley Moore Capito (R-WV), "Bipartisan Duo Continues Promoting Civility Taskforce," press release, April 24, 2007.

56. Mann and Ornstein, *The Broken Branch,* 232.

57. Speech by Mickey Edwards, "Checks and Balances: Perspectives on American Democracy," Center for American Progress and American University, St. Regis Hotel, Washington, D.C., August 31, 2005.

INDEX

ABOUT THE AUTHOR

SUNIL AHUJA is Associate Professor of Political Science at Youngstown State University. He is Editor of the recurrent series *The Roads to Congress*, former coeditor of *Legislative Studies Quarterly*, and Past President of the Northeastern Political Science Association.